THE
HARVEST

RICK JOYNER

PUBLISHED AND DISTRIBUTED BY:

MorningStar Publications, Inc.
8704 Paulston Road
Charlotte, North Carolina 28226

Library of Congress Catalog Card # 89-091635

I.S.B.N. 1-878327-00-3

TABLE OF CONTENTS

INTRODUCTION

To properly understand this vision it must be kept in mind that it represents a GRADUAL unfolding which takes place over a period of time, possibly many years. Though I was not given the timing of these events, it is obvious that some are already beginning to take place. Whether the complete unfolding takes five years or fifty I do not know, but I do know that even if it takes fifty we do not have any time to waste.

This vision came in three parts: the first in September 1987, the second in May 1988, the third in September 1988. Between these dates I received numerous revelations which corroborated and illuminated this vision and which are also included.

Since distributing the summary of the first vision, I have met others who have seen and recorded the same basic vision, in some cases with more clarity and detail. As we have been promised, "Surely the Lord our God does nothing unless He reveals His secret counsel to His servants the prophets (plural)" (AMOS 3:7). Those who foresee these things all seem to have some parts that others do not see, but which do correspond to the others. To be properly received this vision must not be considered exclusive or all inclusive, but one part that must be joined with others to give a complete picture.

This vision ends during the harvest and I do not know at what point in the harvest it ends, or how much more time remains after what I have been allowed to see. This vision is but a cursory depiction of these events.

The scriptures do verify this vision, but I have included few here to leave room for the Lord to speak individually to those who receive it, believing this will make it more meaningful to the reader. Just reading and agreeing with someone else's vision does not necessarily make it revelation to us. It is when the Lord confirms the word that we have our own encounter with Him and it is no longer just someone else's revelation. We must always be like the men of Samaria who came to believe in Jesus, not just because of the testimony of the woman at the well, but because they saw and heard Him for themselves.

1

It is time for judgement to begin, and it begins with the household of God (I PET.4:17). The apostle explained, "But when we are judged, we are disciplined by the Lord in order that we may not be condemned along with the world" (I COR. 11:32). There is no safe place we can go, or anything we can do to escape the coming judgments, EXCEPT to be found in Christ. Jesus is our Ark in Whom we find deliverance. If we are abiding in Him we will be at the right place, and doing the right thing. If there is a central theme that runs throughout this vision, it is that we must now return to our first love and never again be beguiled from the simplicity of devotion to Christ.

All things are to be summed up in Christ (EPH.1:10). As we abide in Him we are fulfilling our purpose and calling in this hour, which is ultimately to bring even every thought in heaven and earth into obedience and harmony with Him. "All things were made through Him and for Him;" JESUS IS THE PURPOSE OF THE CREATION, He IS the plan of God. Jesus is the love and desire and delight of the Father. In all that was made He was looking for His Son; He is looking for His Son in us.

There are a number of redundancies purposely included in this book. These are meant to recall attention to issues which are of the utmost importance.

It is the nature and purpose of prophecy, not to just foretell events, but sometimes to provoke a response to the prediction which results in repentance and/or intercession which can change our destiny and the unfolding events. We see a number of Biblical examples of this, such as when Jonah preached in Nineveh. Even though Jonah did not preach a contingency that Nineveh's overthrow could be averted by repentence, it is implied in every prophecy of judgement. That Nineveh was not overthrown did not make Jonah a false prophet, but was the fruit of a true and anointed prophetic word. Can one envision such a heathen city repenting as it did with the preaching of one Jew, with no signs or miracles attesting to the word, without anointing? There are events contained in this prophecy which CAN BE CHANGED by repentance and intercession. There are also events which cannot and/or will not be changed because of their intricate place in the unfolding of the ultimate purpose of God. These are not revealed here because the Lord wants us to seek Him about all of these events. Our response should be prayer and repentence for both the positive and negative aspects of all that He reveals today that we might be made into vessels fit for His use.

The sequence in which these events are laid out in this prophecy is not necessarily the sequence in which they will occur. Even in Biblical prophecy the sequence of events is often purposely jumbled so that it does not flow in the order in which it is to unfold. This was not done by the Lord to confuse us, but to keep us dependent on Him for interpretation. This keeps us seeking <u>Him</u> and not just understanding. The encounters we have with Him as He gives revelation and knowledge teach us His ways and not just facts. In this way we might preach His message by His Spirit, His heart, not just by the letter.

I pray that as you seek understanding through this vision that you encounter Him, see His glory, and are changed by it in a way that would enable you to worship Him more perfectly in Spirit and truth. Only then can we properly understand His works.

CHAPTER 1

THE HARVEST

Jesus said, "The harvest is the end of the age" (MATT.13: 39). Between now and the end of the age more people will come to know Jesus than have from Pentecost until now. Before the end every village in every nation will have had the gospel preached to them. Every person living will hear His name. The knowledge of the Lord will cover the earth as the waters cover the sea and many whole cities and some entire nations will be converted to Him. The magnitude of what is coming cannot be measured by anything which has ever been before; even the cosmos itself will be electrified with its energy. More than a tithe of all the people who have ever lived, more than one billion souls, will call upon His name in true commitment resulting in true conversion.

This harvest will exceed previous outpourings of the Spirit in a profound way because Jesus will be preached as Lord and not just Savior. During this harvest the gospel will change from "Come and be saved," to "Bow the knee, He is the King." This is the seventh and last trumpet, or message, to be preached. This message will not come in word only, but in power and unprecedented demonstrations of the Spirit.

There is another aspect to the harvest that is the end of the age: the reaping of evil. A harvest is the reaping of all that has been sown. The evil which was sown in man will also come to fruition during this time. While the "wheat" is being gathered, the "tares" will also be gathered into bundles, or unified. However, the gathering of the tares is actually to aid the gathering of the wheat. The separation and distinction between the two seeds will become increasingly visible in the days to come. The "man of sin," or the personification of the "sin of man," will also be fully revealed and understood during the harvest. This is not to be feared; He who is in us is MUCH greater than he who is in the world, and the least of those in the Kingdom of God has more power than all of the anti-Christs. Nevertheless, this evil must be understood.

5

This vision is given to encourage and prepare those who will be laborers in this great work. It includes certain ecclesiastical and world events which relate to this preparation. These are not shared for the purpose of emotional stimulation, but because the information is needed for the church to accomplish its mandate. It is time to awaken, to be sober in spirit, and to give ourselves fully to the purposes for which we have been called. "He died for all, that they who live SHOULD NO LONGER LIVE FOR THEMSELVES, BUT FOR HIM" (II COR.5:15). It is now time for us to walk in a manner worthy of our calling.

Every believer has a specific job to do; we have all been called for a purpose. The Lord wants everyone whose name is written in His Book Of Life to see his own name written, to know that he is known by Him, and to see clearly His plan for their life.

In the coming days, the most powerful army ever assembled will be mustered. This army will not be equipped with guns or swords, but no power in heaven or earth will prevail against it. Its leadership will seem undistinguished, and in some cases invisible, but no human organization has ever equaled its discipline and resolve. This army has been enlisted by the Lord Himself; He will train it and He will lead it. When the battle unfolds its members will march in perfect order, without deviating from their paths or crowding each other, unyielding in their resolve, with the least of them having more power than the greatest of their enemies. This is the army of God envisioned by the prophets, soon to be a reality.

To be numbered in this army will require a training and spiritual discipline exceeding the physical and mental discipline required of elite military units. In relation to this I was shown a war horse. This creature had been wild and easily frightened into spontaneous and uncontrolled reactions. After its training it was not affected by external stimuli. Even as this horse charged into the face of canons, rifles and sabres, he never lost his composure. In the most deafening confusion of battle he was able to feel and respond to the gentle nudge of his master's knees or heels, which directed him to turn or change his pace. This will be the discipline of the coming last day ministry. Regardless of the confusion and noise of the battle, the church will be so in touch with the Master that she will feel and respond to His most gentle nudgings. Just as the war horse not trained in this way would put himself and his rider in jeopardy, those who today do not submit to the Lord's discipline will be in grave danger in the coming days. "TODAY if you hear His voice do not harden your heart."

The Lord has prepared a ministry for this last day which will be the marvel of men and angels. These will not be self-seeking or self-promoting, and most of them will remain unknown to the world and to much of the church. Their works and preaching will stir nations, but many will fade into the crowds and disappear before anyone even knows who they are.

These have no desire to build a ministry, and will not covet fame and fortune. They are "spiritual celibates;" they will not rape the bride. Just as a natural eunuch is given entirely to preparing the bride for the king, and has no desire for her as he is not even able to, these will be completely given to preparing the church for her King. Their whole purpose is to see the King's joy because they are truly His friends. These will follow Him wherever He goes.

While many of their peers have been seeking exposure and promotion for their ministries, these have been quietly preparing themselves just as Jesus did for His first 30 years. While others are advancing in ministry these are retreating. While others are building up these have been digging down, trying to strengthen their foundations and deepen their roots. Not meaning to, and usually grieving over it, these are usually out of harmony with much of the church. These are the ones about which it was said, "We played the flute for you and you did not dance. We sang a dirge for you and you did not mourn."

When the battle unfolds, much of the leadership in the church will have gained their positions through self-promotion and political manipulation. Many who the people consider "generals" will be privates in God's eyes. Some in the lower ranks in the people's eyes will be God's top generals. These will not even seek rank or position in the church at this time, but will quietly, mostly incognito, direct the end time strategy of the church. Their authority will be in their wisdom. Like Stephen, who was but a deacon, but whose wisdom and power lit a fire that set a new course for Christianity, this new breed, without fame or position, will direct the greatest events in history. Though men will never know many of them, the entire host of heaven and hell have known them from the beginning.

Not since Jesus has the enemy feared anyone like he does these selfless messengers of power. Just as he tried to destroy Moses and Jesus by killing the children, his present onslaught through abortion and drugs is a desperate attempt to destroy these before they can mature. Some of them will have been dragged through the dregs of human sin, trauma and despair before they are awakened. They will love much because they were forgiven of much, and delivered of much. As deep as the enemy has been able to get his roots into them, that is how deep the Lord will fill them after their deliverance. Others will have been raised in religious shelter, but the good they know will be from the Tree of Knowledge and not the Tree of Life. Like Saul of Tarsus, these will struggle in religious anguish until their release; then they will be used to put the ax to the root of the tree which has caused all of the death from the beginning. These will shine with the light of the Tree of Life and bring healing to the nations.

The Lord began forming His "body" on the Day of Pentecost. Through the centuries He has continued building this body, adding to it those who overcame in every age. The last members to be added to this body are metaphorically referred to as the "feet." Just as our feet touch the earth while the rest of the body stands erect in the air, the "feet" of the Lord's body will touch the earth but represent the entire body which stands completed in the heavenlies. The scriptures say that all of His enemies will be crushed under His FEET, but these represent all who have gone before them.

When Jesus was asked by what authority He did the works, He asked His inquisitors a question: "Was the baptism of John of God or of men?" This was not an arbitrary question; the answer to this question was the answer to their question. Jesus had credentials exceeding anyone who had

8

ever walked this earth. From the first prophecy given to the woman about her Seed who would crush the serpent, through an unending chain of prophets and righteous men, even through all of the ritual of their own Law, every word had spoken of Him. John stood as the representative of that order who had prepared His way and testified that He was indeed the Lamb of God. To be baptized by John was to acknowledge this testimony of the One who was BORN king.

The "feet" of the body of Christ will carry the credentials for all of those who have gone before them. They will be joined to each other like no other body of people have ever been joined, but they will also be joined to the true believers of all ages who lived and prophesied of this day. As Jesus promised, the things which He did, and even greater things, will be done in His name. His faithful will soon walk in unprecedented power and authority. In the near future we will not be looking back at the early church with envy because of the great exploits of those days, but all will be saying that He certainly did save His best wine for last. The most glorious times in all of history have now come upon us. You who have dreamed of one day being able to talk with Peter, John and Paul, are going to be surprised to find that they have all been waiting to talk to you! You have been chosen to see the harvest, the fruit of the seeds which they were planting.

We have come to the most blessed time to walk with God, but we must not be arrogant. The feet would not be of any use without the rest of the body, and we would not be where we are except for those who laid down their lives before us. When the feet are joined to the rest of the body the whole body will be rejoicing in the triumph of this day, and receiving of its fruit.

Sowing For The Harvest

The nature of spiritual truth can be found in ECCL.3:1, "There is an appointed time for everything..." There is a time to plant and a time to reap, but there will not be a reaping if we have missed the time to plant. The church has had a "reaping mentality" which has caused it to overlook many of the planting seasons. Because of this our harvests have amounted to little more than the gathering of what has grown wild.

Many have not been willing to work unless they could count what they accomplished, to put it in reports, newsletters and books. We like to see immediate results or often we feel like failures. Indeed, many missionaries would lose their support if they didn't produce quick results. Only eternity will tell how much this has cost the church in her effectiveness. The Lord will soon change this mentality in His laborers. Just as the farmer doesn't plant the seed and stand there waiting for fruit, these will have the wisdom to plant knowing that the results of this labor may not be seen for a long time, and may not be seen by them at all. Some will plant, others will water, but God will give and receive the increase.

Even science verifies the Lord's statement that a seed cannot sprout unless it first dies, or goes through a period of dormancy. This is a God-created protective mechanism in the seed which keeps it from sprouting until conditions are right for growth. To sprout, a seed must have the proper amount of water, heat and light. Having two out of three of these will not work. This is to keep the seed from being fooled into thinking it is spring because of a wet warming trend. If these are not accompanied with enough light each day, the seed knows that spring has not really come.

The same is true of spiritual seeds. We may want to see immediate results from our preaching or witnessing, but the Lord will protect the seeds until the conditions are right for growth. Spiritual seeds require the same basic conditions as natural seeds: water, heat and light. Water speaks of the Word of God, of which there must be an abundance. Heat speaks of circumstances, as most have to be in the fire of trials before they will turn to the Lord. Light speaks of Divine revelation which enables us to realize that it is God who is speaking through the Word and circumstances.

Between each great move of God there is a period of quietness in which there appears to be little happening. This is the time for planting. As stated, our "reaping mentality" has caused us to miss many of these planting seasons, but never again; a zeal for sowing seeds is about to sweep the church.

Those seeking to plant for the harvest will be given words of wisdom and words of knowledge for this purpose. Most of these will be subtle, gently arousing questions in those to whom they are given. Others will astonish and profoundly move the recipients. At the proper time both will accomplish their purpose.

To be effective the "revelation gifts" must be used in the wisdom of the Holy Spirit. If we had received a word of knowledge about the woman at the well how many of us would have jumped up and called her an adulteress! Jesus did not. He gently led her in the conversation, and never did rebuke her for her sins. The reality of Who she had encountered more than likely convicted her of the adultery and any other sin. There are times for bold confrontations, such as the Lord had with the Pharisees, but that could have been devastating for this particular woman, or even for Nicodemas, who was himself a Pharisee. One of the least emphasized but most important gifts of the Spirit is the gift of a word of wisdom. This is the supernatural impartation of the mind of Christ into specific situations. This is a more subtle and less spectacular gift than the word of knowledge or the power gifts, but without it the others may be rendered less effective, or even counterproductive in accomplishing God's purposes.

The preaching of Jesus must be in obedience to the Holy Spirit who was given for this reason. The Lord has blessed and used many different strategies and tactics devised by zealous men in the past to reach the lost, but not in the future. Great trials and testings will come upon the church until His laborers are utterly submitted to the movings of the Spirit. This will multiply the effectiveness of His messengers and enable Him to trust them with power and authority never before given to men.

The industrial age disease which requires us to have a formula for everything, which demanded the packaging of the gospel into spiritual laws, is contrary to true evangelism. Our formulas will get a "decision" out of a few, and may actually result in the conversion of some, but often the effect of this type of witness is to inoculate the masses so that they are immune to the true witness, which is an encounter with God. The laborers who are coming will be armed with far more than a recipe for getting a quick decision. "For the kingdom of God does not consist in words but in power" (I COR.4:20), and power is about to come upon the true witnesses after they have been trained.

This is not meant to attack any ministry seeking to bring people into a relationship with Jesus. But we will not be prepared for what is coming if we do not recognize our present condition. Immaturity does have its place. It is acceptable for a two year old to wear diapers. It is a reflection of her immaturity but a two year old is supposed to be immature. In fact, she may even be quite mature for her age. If she were twelve and had this condition there would be a problem! Many ministries and churches are quite immature, but they are where they are supposed to be. The issue is are we growing up? What is soon to be upon us demands our maturity.

The Ingathering

The magnitude of this harvest will ultimately astonish even the most optimistic believers. Congregations of less than a hundred will be adding a thousand believers a week for periods of time. Meetings which begin spontaneously will stir entire cities, continuing until they fill the largest stadiums night after night. The most popular sports will be abandoned in many regions for lack of interest. Whole towns, with populations of thousands, will swarm upon neighboring towns to evangelize them. The news media will be dominated by the harvest until they have fanned the flames throughout the world. News teams will follow apostles like national leaders, recording great miracles which will be shown with unabashed enthusiasm. Some of these individual broadcasts will result in more conversions than Christian networks have during their entire existence.

Large cities will experience periods of "zero crime" as their populations come under the conviction of the Holy Spirit, and the light of the church drives darkness from entire regions. Pornography, prostitution, illegal drugs, abortion and drunkenness will cease to exist in many areas without the passage of a single law. Large factories and businesses will shut down for days at a time so their employees can attend special meetings. Whole nations will give themselves to periods of prayer and fasting. The inflow of new believers will be so great in places those very young in the ministry will find themselves pastoring great multitudes. Some churches will be dividing every few months, not because of conflicts, but because their growth is so great they must keep the size down to what is manageable, with each split resulting in the birth of new congregations.

The Lord will continually be on the minds of the people. Coffee breaks, lunch breaks and siestas will become Bible studies and prayer meetings. Cities will sponsor bonfires for burning pornography, witchcraft and astrological paraphernalia, and illegal drugs. Warlocks, witches, mediums and even mafia chieftains will be bowing the knee to Jesus and entering into salvation with great joy. Street gangs will be sending Bibles and gifts to one another and prisons will become churches which give the Body of Christ some of its greatest teachers.

Miracles which exceed even the greatest Biblical marvels will cause whole nations to acknowledge Jesus. Leaders of some of the most powerful communist countries will be openly confessing the Lord and exhorting their people to follow Him. The visible glory of the Lord will appear upon some for periods of time, and this glory will heal everyone it touches. The pillar of fire that led Israel will not even compare to the intense presence of the Lord in these days. The appearance of angels will be so common they will cease to be related as significant events. The Lord Himself will appear to councils of apostles and elders to give them directives. This will impart a courage and peace which will astonish and gain the respect of even the most vehement opposers. Never has the Lord been as personal and intimate with His people as He will in these days. Believers will be in awe continually, wondering each day what great new things they will see.

One of the most extraordinary characteristics of the harvest will be the youthfulness of the laborers. Teenagers will be the backbone of the revival, preteens some of its greatest evangelists. Young children will cast out demons, heal the sick, raise the dead, divert raging floods with a word. Some will actually take dominion over entire hospitals and mental institutions, healing every patient in them by laying hands on the building. During the harvest the world will know that "the children are for signs and wonders."

Just as the light of the gospel is shining so brightly much of the world will be in its deepest darkness. There will be regions where the peace and love of the Lord reign, and these will become fortresses from which the church will go out and attack the fear and paranoia sweeping the rest of the earth. There will be great defeats following victories, and great victories following defeats. Large cities will be under almost the complete dominion of the Lord. Others will be almost completely in the grips of an evil more terrible than we may presently be able to comprehend. The Lord will never have moved in such great power, but neither will the enemy have ever been so desperate. At the end of the vision both light and darkness are increasing throughout the entire earth.

We must be prepared for this conflict. There will be martyrs during the harvest. In places the church will be almost completely wiped out. But the lives of these martyrs will be seed for a harvest in that same place. Where the enemy makes his most powerful attacks are the very places where the greatest advances of the gospel will be made. Remember that light shines into darkness, it is not the other way around. When you open your shades at night darkness does not come in; light shines out. Light is more powerful than darkness and will always overcome it.

The Fishnet

For the coming harvest the Lord is preparing a great spiritual "fishnet" which will be able to hold the catch that is coming. This net is formed by the linking together of His people. The links in this net are the interrelationships and intercommunication of His people. The stronger the intercommunication and interrelationships, the stronger this net will be. This is not only happening in the local churches among members, but between ministries, congregations and the different streams in the Body of Christ throughout cities, states, and crossing international barriers around the world.

In Ephesians 4:15-16, we see this principle: "... we are to grow up in all aspects into Him, who is the Head, even Christ, from whom the whole body, being fitted and held together by that which every JOINT supplies." A joint is not a part, but it is where two parts come together. There is a great fitting together going on in the Spirit now and it will increase on all levels. With each new joint there will be substantial growth and edification for those who are joined.

The Spirit is compelling pastors to get together with other pastors, prophets with prophets, apostles with apostles, and even whole congregations are beginning to visit and interrelate with other congregations apart from their own circles of emphasis. This is the Lord's doing. Some of these meetings may seem fruitless because of improper agendas but they will bear fruit, there will be links made. Soon the Lord's presence in these meetings will melt all presumption and the facades which separate us from union with Him and each other. His presence will stimulate a worship that brings about Psalm 133 unity; as we anoint the Head with our worship the oil will flow down to the edge of His robes until it covers the entire body.

He is beginning this breakdown of barriers with the leadership because this is where most originate and where they are the strongest. As the walls come down here the entire body will begin flowing together. If the leaders resist this move the Lord will continue through the congregations. These will begin to relate to other members of the body of Christ and their bonds will grow stronger regardless of the opposition or warnings of pastors who resist. This is a move of the Holy Spirit and it cannot be stopped. The pastors and leaders who continue to resist this tide of unity will be removed from their place.

Some who are presently in leadership that resist this move will become so hardened they will become opposers and persecutors of the church. Others will be changed and repent of their hardness of heart, even though, in some cases, their resistance to the Holy Spirit will have disqualified them from leadership. This growing tide of unity in the church will reveal the true nature of those in leadership. Those who have been building for themselves and their own reputations will be threatened by this move which is beyond their control. Those who have been ordained by God, and not just an institution, will become increasingly determined to give up "control" over their people and circumstances, deferring to the Holy Spirit. The "control" they relinquish will be replaced by a spiritual authority grounded in the peace and rest of God. What is coming is beyond any man's ability to control. Only the Holy Spirit can order this work and He is now starting to take His authority.

Because of the magnitude of the "catch" this net will be rent many times and will be in need of constant mending. Much of the discord now taking place in the church is used by the Lord to prepare those whose task in the harvest will be almost exclusively devoted to the mending and binding of this great net. These peacemakers will have a great part in building this net and will have a major impact on the effectiveness of the entire revival. Those that seem to always find themselves in the middle of conflicts should be encouraged with the knowledge that they are being prepared for a great work. Even with the awesome presence of the Lord there will still be bickering and disputing among the disciples, just as there was among the twelve. Even great apostles like Paul and Barnabas allowed issues to divide them, and it will happen at times with even the greatest men of God. But the net will get mended, and become even stronger where it was broken.

Some who were used greatly of God in the past have become too rigid in doctrinal emphasis, or are too entangled with spiritual "Ishmaels", to participate in this revival. Some of these will try to join the work but their interrelationships will be so superficial they will quickly be torn from the net by the first catch. Those who are linked together by doctrine or who gather around personalities will quickly be torn away. Only those who are joined by and through Jesus alone will stand the pressure this harvest will bring upon the church (Col.1:17).

The redemption of so many will bring much joy but they will come with problems which bring enormous stress to congregations and ministers. The cords of unity must be very strong to stand this pressure. Those who have not learned to take the Lord's yoke, instead of carrying the burdens themselves, will be overwhelmed. Entering the Sabbath rest of the Lord will become a major emphasis in preparation for the harvest. Heed this word!

A large number who are now considered Christians have never been led to the Lord. They were led to the church, to a personality, or to a doctrine or emphasis. Some of these will think they are important links in the net but will actually become part of the harvest, starting over again on the proper Foundation, Jesus. This will include a number of well known ministers and pastors. Their humility in this will lead multitudes to question and strengthen their own relationship to the Lord. This will do much to undergird and encourage the entire body of Christ.

Denominations, extra-local fellowships and circles of emphasis will begin disbanding and severing their ties, even those that were ordained by God for a season, in order to be a part of this great net. For some these ties will just be ignored or forgotten until they have passed away, almost without notice, because of the greater intensity and substance of this new move. For others it will be a very painful rending as they are persecuted and rejected by those who do not understand. The pain of these broken relationships will not last long for those who must endure them; a true church life that has been the desire of Christians since Pentecost will soon be realized by those willing to pay the price for it.

Some leaders will actually disband their organizations as they realize they are no longer relevant to what God is doing. Others will just leave them behind to disband themselves. Ultimately, all circles of ministry or influence with individual identities will dissolve into a single identity of simply being Christians for all who become part of this harvest. The present streams and movements will eventually flow into the one River of Life. When this happens there will be nothing left that can stop or even hinder the force with which it flows. It will sweep about like a great flood that carries away everything in its path. Every religious fortress and lie which exalts itself against the knowledge of God will be swept away

17

by this great river. As the different streams of light begin flowing together their power will become concentrated like the greatest laser from which there is no protection. The cloak behind which every religious impostor hides will be stripped away so that they are apparent to all. This light will ultimately become too bright for any darkness to hide within the church.

Single presbyteries will form over cities and localities. These will be made up of pastors and leaders from all different backgrounds. Their unity in purpose, as well as that of the various congregations, will be a marvel to the world that is itself degenerating into chaos and paranoia.

THE TRAVAIL OF THE SPIRIT

When declaring events which would signal the end of the age the Lord noted that these were "the beginning of birth pangs" (MATT.24:8). The harvest and accompanying events will unfold just as travail comes upon a woman in labor. That is, the contractions begin suddenly, but at first they are infrequent and relatively light, but the closer to the birth the more intense and the more frequent they become. The first contractions signaling the end of the age actually occurred several hundred years ago, beginning with the Reformation. Over two hundred years passed before there was another, then a hundred years, until now the time between them is down to decades. Soon it will be just years; and each one is becoming more intense.

In labor, the contractions actually push the baby into the birth canal, while opening the cervix to allow entry into the world. With each spiritual contraction, that which the Lord is bringing to birth was pushed further down the canal, and the way was opened a little wider for its eventual manifestation.

During childbirth, the mother can complicate and endanger herself and the child because her natural tendencies are to do the opposite of what she should be doing at each stage of the process. This is why education through "natural" childbirth classes has enabled mothers to give birth with much less, and in some cases, no pain. They teach the mother how to resist her tendencies and do what will actually help the process. If the church is to flow with the birth process we too must resist some of our natural tendencies. During the "transition" stage, when the baby is entering the birth canal, the mother usually goes through severe disorientation, often wanting to quit right there and forget the whole thing, though this is of course impossible. Physicians specializing in natural childbirth have found that it helps immensely for the mother to have a "focal point" on which to concentrate during this time. It is also essential for the mother to heed the instructions of the labor "coach" (usually the husband) and obey them regardless of her pain or feelings.

The Lord used "birth pangs" to describe the unfolding of these times and it is hard to imagine a more appropriate metaphor. Unfortunately, the church, being in much ignorance of the actual process through which she is going, has continued to follow her natural instincts instead of revelation. This has caused her to strive counter-productively through much of the proess, leaving her now weary and expended as we enter the most critical stages of delivery. Never has it been more important for us to have our focal point and be in tune with the instructions of our Husband. If we don't we can bring grave complications upon ourselves.

The Restoration Of Ministries

Beginning with Luther, each spiritual contraction resulted in a major, basic Christian truth being restored to the church, as well as one of the five ministries given for the equipping of the saints, as listed in Ephesians 4. During the Middle Ages apostles, prophets, evangelists, pastors and teachers were unrecognized and had ceased to function in the church, except on isolated and rare occasions. The church was then dominated by a false priestcraft, but with the restoration of truth to the church there also had to come a restoration of true ministry.

With the beginning of The Reformation the PASTOR was restored to recognized ministry. Over two hundred years later, with the Wesleys, the EVANGELIST was restored and attained general recognition and acceptance. The Pentecostal and Latter Rain revivals began the restoration of the gifts of the Holy Spirit, but it was not until the Charismatic Renewal that the TEACHING ministry was fully restored. Teaching was the primary emphasis, and a much greater anointing came upon this ministry during that movement. Until then most of those with a teaching ministry were relegated to seminaries or seminars. Now this ministry is truly being incorporated into the life of the local church, resulting in the building up of the whole body.

20

The next spiritual contraction will bring about the restoration and recognition of the PROPHETS. We will see the prophetic ministry become the primary focus of attention during the next few years as a much greater anointing comes upon this ministry than has been seen since Biblical times. Just as there were some pastors, evangelists and teachers in the Body of Christ before their ministries were fully restored, there have been some prophets in the church; they just have not received the understanding, anointing, and acceptance that they soon will.

The church has been well prepared for the restoration of this ministry. The Body of Christ is now aware that it must have a much greater clarity of vision and revelation of the Divine purpose in the days to come. The prophet is the eye of the body (see IS.29:10) and when the eye is single, or unified, the whole body will be full of light. We are promised this unity of vision in IS.52:8, "Listen! Your watchmen (one of the Biblical designations for prophets) lift up their voices, they will shout joyfully TOGETHER; for they will see eye to eye when the Lord restores Zion." Those who are emerging with a true prophetic mantle will be joined in a union which is unprecedented in this ministry.

The Charismatic movement was sidetracked and stifled by well meaning, but misguided, men who sought to bring order and unity through human initiatives and organizations. The same will be true with the restoration of the prophetic ministry. These prophetic organizations will ultimately bring as much confusion and disorientation as was afflicted upon the Charismatic Renewal. We must understand that every time the Lord plants wheat that the enemy is going to come and plant tares. We must not disregard the wheat just because tares have been sown in the midst of it. The tares will soon be gathered into recognizable "bundles" of mere human organization to be cast into the fires of judgment now being kindled in the world.

We must understand that one may be a false teacher or prophet AND STILL BE A BORN AGAIN BROTHER IN THE LORD! The Lord Jesus Himself warned of this when He said, "For many will come in My name, saying, 'I am the Christ,' and will mislead many" (MATT.24:5). Some have interpreted this as indicating that these would come saying that THEY were the Christ, but that is not what He said. He said that they would come saying He, JESUS, was indeed the Christ but they would still be deceivers. One becomes a false teacher or prophet when he tries to walk in a ministry to which he has not been ordained by God. This does not mean that these are not redeemed believers, they are just deceived and therefore deceive others.

The Lord went on to say that there would be false Christs and false prophets who would arise and show great signs and wonders, in an attempt to mislead even the elect, or true prophets, etc... There will be tares sown among the wheat, but there would be no counterfeit if that which is true did not also exist. There would be no counterfeit money if there was not true money. The only reason the enemy brings false signs and wonders is because there are real signs and wonders.

The Lord has told us how we may distinguish the false from the real in JOHN 7:18, "He who speaks from himself seeks his own glory (literal "recognition"); but he who is seeking the glory of the One who sent him, he is true and there is no unrighteousness in him." Regardless of how tearfully one uses the name of Jesus, self-seeking and self-promotion will always surface in those who are self-appointed. Regardless of how much one talks of giving all the glory to God, those who are seeking their own recognition are speaking from themselves, at best.

Some of the most destructive false prophets will be those who were called as true prophets, but have let self-seeking gain entrance to their ministry. These may be gifted with the true spiritual gifts. "The gifts and callings of God are irrevocable" (ROM.11:29). The Lord does not take back His gifts even when we become unfaithful. He remains faithful even when we do not. That is why so many effective ministries have fallen into immorality, drunkenness and other forms of corruption, but the gifts would continue to function in their ministry. That is why the Lord told us to judge by FRUIT, not gifts. Gifts are given but fruit must be grown. The decade of the eighties should have awakened us to this important fact. Unfortunately many will not heed this warning. Paul marveled at how the Corinthians could follow those who "slapped them in the face," and could reject him who poured out his life for them. Carnal men will always respond more readily to carnal strength because the natural man does not understand the ways of the Spirit.

The spiritual contraction bringing the restoration of the prophetic ministry to the church will be so great many will believe that it is in fact the harvest. Multitudes will be streaming to the Lord as this will be one of the greatest revivals in history. These millions who come in are not the harvest, but are called as laborers for the true harvest which is yet to come. These multitudes must not just be herded into "sheep pens," but must be thoroughly equipped for service in the harvest.

There will be another contraction during which a true APOSTOLIC authority will be restored and recognized within the advancing church. It is noteworthy that these ministries are being restored in the reverse order in which they were lost to the church. The early church began in a place of light and regressed into darkness. The last day church is coming out of the darkness and progressing toward increasing light. This light will increase until the fullness of day comes with the full revelation of Jesus.

These ministries did exist in the church before their restoration, to a degree, but with the contraction which restored their recognition came a commissioning restoring a greater anointing and clarity of function. Just as there were some evangelists before Wesley, and teachers before the Charismatic Renewal, there are some prophets and apostles in the church today. But even the most significant of these are not yet walking in the full authority of their offices.

The prophets soon to be commissioned will greatly exceed in gifts and authority that which is presently accepted as prophetic ministry, and ultimately, that which has even historically existed. The glory of the latter house will be greater than the former. This is not to imply that the house is greater, as in fact, the latter house (temple) was inferior to the former, but the glory to be revealed in it is greater. This has nothing to do with the righteousness or worthiness of either the early church or the last day church, but is entirely related to the purpose of God for the times.

A power and authority is about to be given to some which will exceed all precedents. This is to fulfill the Lord's promise that even greater works than He had done would be performed. Those who walk in this will not be perfect men, and they will make mistakes just like their Biblical counterparts. There will be a number who will demonstrate unprecedented revelation and power. There will be many others, like the companies of prophets who attended Samuel and Elijah, who will seem average by comparison, but who at times will accomplish the most extraordinary individual exploits. Some of these will spend their entire lives preparing to give just one word to the church or to a nation, with that one word accomplishing as much as others have in a lifetime of service.

The advancing church has gone from the Protestant gospel, to the Evangelical, to the Pentecostal, to the Charismatic. Each move felt they had the "full gospel", but none did. NEITHER WILL THE NEXT MOVE. Our understanding of even the most basic doctrines is about to expand dramatically, but will still fall short of the apostolic faith. This will not be fully restored until the apostolic ministry has been FULLY restored. With the restoration of the prophetic ministry, a vision of the apostolic faith will be imparted.

We Are In Labor Until Christ Is Formed

For all of its problems and shallowness, great truths were restored to the church through the Charismatic Renewal. Many of these truths were carried to extremes and error because the church allowed them to become the focal point in place of the only One upon Whom we must keep our attention. This led to disorientation, and it always will. The Way is not a principle or formula, but a Person. Walking in Truth is not just assimilating and agreeing with certain spiritual facts, but following a Person. Deception is not just misunderstanding doctrines or principles; it is not being in His will. We can know all truth accurately and still be disobedient. Our goal is more than just knowing the book of the Lord; it is knowing the Lord of the book. We can memorize the Bible but not know the Word Himself. Jesus is Truth and He is the summation of all the individual truths that were restored, or will be restored in the coming move. We must never again allow ourselves to be distracted from the simplicity of devotion to Christ Himself. Unfortunately, many will once again lose THE focal point and give their whole attention to new truths and emphasis. New "streams" with great new truths and dynamic ministries will add much life to the church, before some of them result in even greater disorientation than in the Charismatic Renewal. Some who were so fooled and distracted during previous moves of the Holy Spirit will not be fooled again, but will be used to give strength and stability during this time.

When apostolic authority is commissioned it will signal the end of the transition stage of our travail. Then the final stage which results in the birth of the end time ministry will commence. In natural childbirth, it is during this stage that a remarkable clarity of purpose returns to the mother, and a strength, which even in "natural" childbirth seems supernatural. This is the time to push until the child comes forth. The restored apostolic faith will so energize the church with resolve that the pains will be forgotten. The reason for centuries of travail, and six millenniums of sacrifice and hope, will then be seen with our own eyes.

With the restoration of apostolic ministry the diverse vision of the church will then be concentrated like a laser upon the Lord Jesus Himself. All things are to be summed up in Him as He IS the whole Purpose of God. The depths of the wisdom and knowledge of God that are found in Him will be revealed and all eyes will be turned upon His glory. Just as light concentrated becomes awesome power in the laser, this will result in power being released in the church.

At this time, all true seekers who were distracted from the River of Life by the little tributaries which feed it, will return to that River never to be distracted again. The Head will finally be joined to the body. Then we will worship in Spirit and Truth.

For nearly two thousand years the Son of Man has been seeking a place to lay His head, a place where He can be the Head. A primary function of the apostolic ministry is the restoration of Jesus as the Head of His church. As this becomes a reality the church will become the greatest demonstration of order and harmony ever witnessed in human affairs. Like the most disciplined and athletic human body, the level of cooperation between ministries, churches and every individual who serves His name, will be the marvel of the world, confounding the greatest thinkers of the day. Without human organization the flow and interchange of ministry will be breathtaking in its precision.

When an evangelist or apostle plants in an area, with perfect timing, others will appear to water those seeds. Seeds will not get planted which do not get watered; and seeds will not be watered which have not been planted. There will be a great deal of interchange and fellowship between ministries, but directives and strategy will not come from mere human planning or computer systems, but by the Holy Spirit. The prophetic word will be flowing with purity and accuracy unsurpassed in church history. Major conferences of the apostles and elders will be convened with no invitations issued, nor a word being passed about it. The Holy Spirit will speak to each who is to attend and He will preside. The Lord Himself will be directing the harvest of the world like the most perfectly managed farm.

The Lord's direction of His work will include even the smallest details. When His teams need capital, food, or other resources they will not even have to ask before it is provided. When Bibles or other materials are needed they will arrive. When a body of believers needs instruction the right teacher will be passing through with perfect timing. There is no computer system or organization known to man that can match the efficiency and timing with which the Lord will direct the harvest. This will all be even more remarkable because of the increasing chaos into which the world will be degenerating during this time.

To prepare for this a great emphasis of the Spirit will be knowing the Lord's voice. The discipline of the Spirit upon those who are being prepared for this last day ministry will be most severe. The consequences of being insensitive to the Spirit in our affairs will become increasingly dramatic and immediate. Christians will find themselves no longer able to get away with the casual manner in which they have previously walked and lived. Presumption that seemed to have little or no effect on us in the past will soon bring sobering retribution.

As the hand of the Lord becomes obvious in the direction of His ministry teams, missionary societies and ministries will begin disbanding their own planning organizations to become completely dependent on the Holy Spirit's guidance. Some organizations will remain and will be used in the disbursement of information, teaching and assisting the interchange throughout the church, but direction and guidance will increasingly become the domain of the Holy Spirit alone.

As stated, all of these events will unfold like birth pangs coming upon a woman. There will be times of great intensity and advancement in the church followed by periods of rest. There will be times of upheaval in the world followed by times of relative peace. There will be a different timing for different places. One city may be experiencing great revival while the next is not. When the Spirit is poured out on the second the first may be quiet. There will be great persecution upon the church in one part of the world while others will be enjoying peace and favor. Because of this it is even more critical that every church and every individual be hearing from the Lord for themselves.

There are some general patterns which the whole church and the whole earth will be moving towards, though at different paces. The church will be increasing in light and power; the world will be sinking into unprecedented darkness. As the true church grows in faith and clarity of vision, the earth will be swept with wave after wave of paranoia. This will increase until no government on earth will be able to control its people. Mobs, sometimes numbering hundreds of thousands, will be sweeping about destroying everything in their path. Plagues, natural disasters and conflicts will bring about such loss of life that it will be impossible to bury the dead. Men will be desperately seeking anyone to take authority for protection, but no one will be willing. The remaining governments will be little more than gangs who have banded together to protect their own interests.

The vision ends with increasing darkness and destruction in the world, and increasing glory and harvest in the church.

It is futile to speculate about what takes place after this, or impose my own doctrinal understandings of following events. Soon the prophetic vision of the church will increase dramatically. Those who are obedient seekers of the Lord and His purposes will not be surprised or overcome by events or circumstances.

Equipping The Saints

A great task lies ahead for the entire church. We have much to do to prepare ourselves for what is coming. As wonderful as it will be to witness the harvest, it will bring enormous stress upon the church. The Lord wants every new convert properly cared for. This will be impossible without the grace and strength of the Lord, but we must also understand that those He has called to responsibility will give an account. We must prepare with earnest. Every believer is called to ministry; and every single one will be needed. It is imperative that each one find their proper place in the body, begin to function in it, and be able to teach others to do the same. Our commission is to: "Go therefore and MAKE DISCIPLES (not just converts) of ALL NATIONS (not just individuals), baptizing them in the name of the Father and the Son and the Holy Spirit, teaching them to observe ALL that I commanded you" (MATT.28:19-20). This is our mandate. He is now enlisting those who will lay aside every encumbrance, and the entanglements of everyday affairs, to do all things for the sake of His gospel.

Those in positions of leadership who are just feeding themselves, and not properly preparing the saints for their service, will soon be severely disciplined or removed from their place. The church does not exist to provide for the ministry; the ministry exists to prepare the church to do the ministry. One of the most frequently preached scriptures over the last few decades is EPH.4:11-12: "He gave some as apostles, and some as prophets, and some as evangelists, and some as pastors and teachers, FOR THE EQUIPPING OF THE SAINTS FOR THE WORK OF SERVICE", yet almost nowhere is this being accomplished.

28

Some works are preparing some of the people for some parts of the ministry, but where are ALL being equipped? Paul declared to the Corinthian church that "the testimony of Christ was CONFIRMED in you SO THAT YOU WERE NOT LACKING IN ANY GIFT" (I COR.6-7).

Gifts are not toys, they are tools for accomplishing the work of the Spirit. Those who function in the gifts and ministries of the Spirit have simply become channels through whom the Lord may reach to touch the needs of His people. Jesus was THE Apostle, THE Prophet, THE Evangelist, THE Pastor and THE Teacher. He functioned in all of the gifts of the Spirit. When He ascended and gave gifts to men, He was in fact giving Himself to men. We cannot recognize a teacher by how well he can expound the scriptures, or articulate sound doctrine, but we must see our Teacher in them. We cannot recognize a true pastor by his degrees, or even by who may have commissioned him, but only by seeing our Shepherd in him. The testimony of Christ is confirmed when no gifts are lacking as that testifies that we have made room for the complete work of Christ in our midst.

We must wake up to our true condition, repent of our disobedience, or we will be removed and our callings given to those who will bear the fruit. For all of the preaching and teaching on equipping the saints it is not getting done. Knowing the truth has not resulted in our walking in truth. This does not bring a blessing, it brings judgement.

As the apostle stated, all of the equipping ministries are given for the equipping of the saints to do the work of the ministry. Even the evangelist, who we tend to think of as sent to the lost, has the primary function of equipping the saints for evangelism, because the whole church is called to that work. If the evangelist is not producing other evangelists and a spirit of evangelism in the church he is not accomplishing his primary function. The same is true of the prophet. His primary function is to equip the saints to speak for God. This does not mean that all will function in the office of prophet, but anyone may be used of God to prophesy, to have visions, dreams, etc... Even the pastor is not just called to guide the people, but to reproduce in the church the Spirit of the Shepherd that we would all become our brother's keepers. No ministry is truly bearing fruit unless it is REPRODUCING "after its own kind."

There is more than enough ministry to go around. We must not be threatened by others who start to walk in our ministries, even if they are more effective than we are. The most perfect type of true spiritual ministry is found with John the Baptist. His whole purpose was to prepare the way for Jesus, to testify of Him, and then to be willing to decrease as He increased. This is why a man who performed no miracles, expounded no new truths and left no institution, was called by the Son Of God "the greatest man ever born of woman." This is the nature of those who are true friends of the bridegroom.

The whole church is called to be an apostle (one sent by God), a prophet (one who speaks for God), and evangelist (bearer of the gospel), a shepherd (our brother's keeper) and a teacher (able to instruct others in the ways of God).

Forsake Not The "Assembling"

The Biblical admonition to "forsake not the assembling" was not just referring to meetings, but the assembling of the Body of Christ together into a unit. The Lord sees only one church. He does not recognize the many divisions we have created. Many of these divisions are brought about because of the fears of weak leaders in their masked attempt to preserve their own dominions and identities. The Lord's people are going to be freed from the spirit of heresy which emphasizes differences instead of our common purpose. A severe judgment is coming upon all who separate instead of join, who are in fact building for themselves instead of Him. This includes individuals, local churches, as well as denominations and the different streams flowing within the church. Satan came to divide and destroy. The fundamental purpose of the Kingdom of God is synthesis, the joining together to form one whole. But we must understand that this synthesis will never be accomplished through human agency; it can come only by the Spirit.

Presently there are a number of different "streams" in the

body of Christ, each with its own different leadership and emphasis. A few are not a part of any one stream but have found the River, where they receive from every stream, but resist the concentration on individual truths or emphasis. Some individuals are looking for the River, but are continually distracted by the different streams, and spend much of their energy just jumping from one to the other. The streams are flowing much faster than the River because they are not as deep. Presently the different streams are in the Lord's purpose, but ultimately all of them will flow together into the one River. At that time this River will swell to become an irresistible force before which no other religion, philosophy, or doctrine can stand.

The body of Christ is presently like the designing of a giant airplane. There are groups of engineers working on each system: one group designing the landing gear, another the engines, another the wings, etc... Most of the engineers can only see and understand their part, which is all they need to understand at this time. Only a few know the plans for the entire plane; and these are committed to the task of being sure that all of the different systems and parts will interface properly when it is time to fit them together. The work of those few who are committed to the interfacing will not be evident until the day the plane is completed and rolled out for display. Then everyone will see their section as essential to the whole, but also as just one little part.

In this same way, those in the different streams have been accomplishing their purpose. Most did not need to see the whole plan. The day has now come for the interfacing to begin. This must happen if any are to be of use. What good would any part of the plane be without the rest of it? The Lord is now beginning to send forth those who see the entire plan. These are working to establish interrelations between the different streams so when the time comes the "wing" will fit properly with the "fuselage," etc...

It is time for interchange to begin, but we must be careful not to force a mating of the sections before they're ready. The Lord has not allowed the different sections of this plane to come together yet because there are still men in leadership who would try to fly it, and He will be its only pilot.

As this interchange begins we must understand that every part will not be directly joined to every other part. The arm must be joined to the shoulder, not the hip, etc... Ultimately all of the parts will be joined, but many will be joined THROUGH other parts, possibly not having much of a direct relationship. It can be a futile waste of time for us to try to join with every other stream in the church. We must be sensitive to give ourselves only to the relationships the Lord is establishing for us.

The dismantling of organizations and disbanding of some works will be a positive and exhilarating experience for the faithful servants. They will not be just leaving something behind, they will be going on to a much greater work. Those who have fallen to worship the work of God more than the God of the work will have trouble, but most of these too will be set free by the tremendous anointing which is coming.

Beware Of Stumbling Blocks

Many who feel called to attack and tear down the old will NOT be sent from God. There will be "stumbling blocks" circulating in the church who will cause confusion and some destruction from time to time. They will perceive themselves as prophets sent to judge and deliver, but they will in fact be sent by the evil one to divide and destroy. Those serving in leadership must trust their discernment and must REMOVE the stumbling blocks.

To be distinguished from the stumbling blocks, the Lord will raise up a great company of prophets, teachers, pastors and apostles who will have the spirit of Phinehas. Just as the son of Eleazar could not tolerate iniquity in the camp of the Lord, this "ministry of Phinehas" will save congregations, and at times cities and nations, from the plagues that will be sweeping the earth (See NUM.25:1-13). They will be moved by the jealousy of the Lord for the purity of His people. They will be sent to save and preserve the work of the Lord, not to tear down like the stumbling blocks.

As part of the Lord's preparation for bringing the church together, there will be an increasing emphasis on walking in sanctification. This is to be distinguished from the legalistic devotion to externals, the decrees the apostle warned about such as, "Do not handle, do not taste, do not touch" (GAL. 2:21). We are exhorted to, "Pursue peace with all men, and the sanctification WITHOUT WHICH NO ONE WILL SEE THE LORD" (HEB. 12:14). Sin separates; it separates us from God and from each other. The Lord will no longer tolerate the lusts of the flesh, the conniving of the soul or the pollution of spirit which has dominated His people. His judgement upon these things is coming with severity just as the prophet Malachi warned:

"For behold, the day is coming, burning like a furnace, and all the arrogant and every evildoer will be like chaff; and the day that is coming will set them ablaze," says the Lord of Hosts, "so that it will leave them neither root or branch."

But for you WHO FEAR MY NAME the Sun of Righteousness will rise with healing in its wings (lit."rays"); and you will go forth and skip about like calves from the stall.

And you will tread down the wicked, for they shall be ashes under the soles of your feet on the day which I am preparing," says the Lord of Hosts (MAL.4:1-3).

False Unity Movements

There will be unity movements started which are not of the Holy Spirit. Some of these will bring increased division and confusion to the church. Some of these will have been originated by deceivers seeking control and coming in the spirit of anti-Christ. Some will be started by true believers who have foreseen what is to come, but will be deluded into thinking they are the chosen vessels to bring it about. There will be so much confusion born out of these false movements that for a time the body of Christ will get sick of the very word "unity."

There will be many relatively small unity movements

resulting in discord, but there will be one great and significant movement which will ultimately become the greatest persecutor of the advancing church. This movement will be a marriage of catholics, protestants, evangelicals, pentecostals, charismatics and third wave Christians. This movement will gain momentum after a period of great humiliation for the church (this is elaborated on in later chapters). It will have all of the appearance of being God's vehicle for re-establishing the credibility of the church when in fact it will be the primary vehicle for anti-Christ forces trying to thwart the harvest.

True unity will not come through any person or movement seeking to bring about unity. It will NOT come through ecumenical movements, political compromises, or the attempt by men to bring about unity, regardless of how noble these may seem. As a reformer once said: "Spiritual men do not need a covenant; unspiritual men cannot keep one." Unity will not even come about through persecution. As history testifies, persecution will cause Christians to lay aside differences for a season, but as soon as the persecution is lifted they again quickly separate. The unity the Spirit is bringing about will weather all conditions and environments because it will not be dependent on environment, but on the Spirit.

What is coming will go beyond human contracts and political agreements. As the Lord prayed in JOHN 17:22: "The GLORY which thou hast given Me I have given to them; that they may be one, just as We are one." The only thing which can bring about true unity is the Glory of the Lord Himself. Those who have exalted themselves will be humbled. Those who have humbled themselves He will exalt. Those seeking to be first will be made last. Those content to be last will be made first.

The unity of the Spirit will only come when we behold the glory of the Lord. As Isaiah testified, "Darkness will cover the earth, and deep darkness the peoples, but THE LORD WILL RISE UPON YOU, AND HIS GLORY WILL APPEAR UPON YOU" (IS.60:2). In the Lord's own prayer for the unity of His church He stated, "The GLORY which Thou hast given Me I have given to them; THAT THEY MAY BE ONE JUST AS WE ARE ONE" (JOHN 17:22). When the church beholds the glory of the Lord, which it will soon do, like the twenty-four elders in Revelation 4:10-11, all crowns will be cast at His feet. Who could presume glory or position in His presence? When we see the Lamb as He is, our pettiness and pretentions will be causing all of us to grovel for mercy, and to repent for the things we have done to injure or divide His people.

Those who enter into the unity of the Spirit will not even be aware of it; their attention will not be on the church and what she is attaining, but on the Lord Himself. The advancing church is soon to rise above worshipping the temple of the Lord to worship the Lord of the temple. This will bring about the true unity.

There has been a fundamental deception promulgated throughout the body of Christ. This deception has sought to focus our attention on who we are in Christ instead of Who He is in us. We do need to know who we are in Him, but when that becomes our emphasis we will never become who He has called us to be. We are not changed by seeing ourselves. It is by beholding His glory that we are changed into His image, which is the image the church is called to bear.

We would do well to comply with the Biblical simplicity for church life and structure. But let us understand that neither the Lord nor the apostolic authors of scripture left us with a clear formula for church structure--purposely! To have done so would have robbed the church of the very life force that indeed makes her the church--Christianity is not a formula; it is a relationship with Christ. The church is not the pattern for the church; Jesus is the pattern for the church. The unity of the church will never come from everyone finally deciding to do everything the same way; it will only come when we all start following the same One.

CHAPTER 3

JUDGEMENT BEGINS

For it is time for judgement to begin with the household of God (I PET.4:17).

But when we are judged, we are disciplined by the Lord in order that we may not be condemned along with the world (I COR.11:32).

The Greek word translated "judgement" in I PET.4:17 quoted above, is "krisis", from which we derive our English word "crisis". Peter was saying that the crisis which is to come upon the world would come upon the church first. This is not for punishment, or condemnation; it is to purify the the church so she will be found standing on a sure foundation when judgement comes upon the world, "in order that we may not be condemned along with the world." It is so that we may be the light we are called to be when the world enters her greatest time of darkness. We cannot pull any one else out of the quicksand unless we ourselves are on solid ground.

One of the definitions for crisis is "the point in a disease in which it is determined if a patient will live or die." This is a good explanation of the judgement the church, and then the world, is about to go through. Everything which can be shaken will be; everything that is not gold, silver, or precious stones will be burned. "Each man's work will become evident; for the DAY will show it, because it is to be revealed with fire; and the fire itself will test the quality of each man's work" (I COR. 3:13). The judgement coming will separate the wheat from the tares in the church, and in the individuals who remain in the church. There is not a Christian who will not be humbled by this fire.

There will not be one who can stand in what is coming except by God's grace. But His grace will be sufficient for all who call upon Him. He will give us His power and His wisdom. This fire will also judge those who presume upon false

37

grace, which is the presumption that He will continue to overlook our irresponsibility and sin. He is coming to judge sin and condemn it in all of its forms. Those who have heard His words, but have not acted on them, will be washed away with the storm. Let us not be like the foolish virgins who did not keep oil in their lamps, presuming that they could get some when the bridegroom came. Those who are so foolish will find themselves locked out.

Before the fire is fully poured out, the Lord will send a clear warning to His people so that we can judge ourselves before He must judge us. It is better to fall on the Rock and be broken than to have the Rock fall on us and be ground into powder. He disciplines those whom He loves, and this judgment is coming because He loves us. The storm will come upon every house, but those who are hearing His words AND ACTING ON THEM, will have built on the Rock and their houses will stand. Those who live in such houses need not fear the storms. If we have excessive fear about these things we must not let it drive us to despair, but to DO SOME-THING about our spiritual condition.

Therefore, let everyone who is godly pray to Thee in a time when Thou mayest be found; surely in a flood of great waters they shall not reach Him (PS.32:6).

We have been promised that if we seek the Lord we will find Him, but it will be too late to save our "houses" if we wait until the flood is upon us. We are choosing today both the judgment and the glory which will come to us.

As a prophetic message, Jesus was crucified between two thieves who represented "yesterday" and "tomorrow." One of the robbers was in bondage to his past and to all of the evil he had done; the other had his attention on the future, saying: "Lord, WHEN you come into your kingdom..." The Lord corrected his emphasis when He said "TODAY, you will be with Me in Paradise" (LUKE 23:43).

It is apparent from the scriptures that the Lord did not go that day to Paradise, but into the depths of the earth. What did He then mean? There is a revelation in knowing Him TO-DAY that touches eternity. Truly, yesterday no longer exists, and neither does tomorrow; the only thing that exists is the Present. Paradise must be found in the present; it is not some futuristic pie in the sky, but a present reality. We must learn from our past, and have a vision for the future, but we are not to live in them. That's why the exhortations are "TODAY, if you hear His voice, do not harden your hearts" (HEB.4:7), and "At the acceptable time I listened to you, and on the day of salvation I helped you, behold NOW is the acceptable time, behold NOW is the day of salvation" (II COR.6:2). More important than knowing the future is abiding in Him TODAY. That's why when Moses asked what name He would be known by He said "I AM," not I WAS, or I WILL BE.

If we are to know Him we must know Him in the Present. The same two metaphorical thieves between whom the Lord was crucified may well have stolen more of the life and power from the church than anything else. We must not let them steal any more. It does not matter how long we have known the Lord, how many times we have read the Bible, how many others we have led to Christ; what matters is if we are abiding in Him TODAY. Neither does it matter how we failed yesterday, how far we backslid, even how we may have denied Him; if we repent, TODAY can be the day of our salvation, TODAY we can establish our lives upon the Rock. Our eternity will be decided TODAY! This vision is given to prepare us for future events, but this knowledge will not do us any good if it does not change our life TODAY.

Those who know the word of the Lord will not be saved by that knowledge; we must be doers of the Word. Many have come to know the way. A few more go on to know truth, but not many come to know Him as their LIFE, and that is what He came to give us. The Way is not a path or a formula, but a Person. The Truth is not an array of certain spiritual facts, but a Person. We don't know the true Way or the Truth if we do not also know Him as our Life. Christianity is not an assimilation of or agreement with certain principles and facts, it is a relationship. That relationship alone can prepare us for what is to come, regardless of how accurately we may foresee the future. The ONLY escape from the judgment is to be found IN CHRIST. The most accurate knowledge of truth or coming events will not help us if we're not abiding in Him.

The bane of Christianity has been the acceptance of rituals for reality, form for substance, concepts and formulas for Life. We must each determine to cultivate a relationship with the Lord that is real and profound; a relationship that is the consuming and undivided concentration of our hearts.

A storm is soon coming upon the entire world, after which only those houses which were built upon the rock will remain ... "HE HAS PROMISED, SAYING, 'YET ONCE MORE WILL I SHAKE NOT ONLY THE EARTH, BUT ALSO THE HEAVEN.' AND THIS EXPRESSION, 'YET ONCE MORE,' DENOTES THE REMOVING OF THOSE THINGS WHICH CAN BE SHAKEN, AS OF CREATED THINGS, IN ORDER THAT THOSE THINGS WHICH CANNOT BE SHAKEN MAY REMAIN," (Heb.12: 26-27). This judgement is to remove that which is not of Him, but it is also for the purpose of establishing and purifying that which is of Him, so that it can remain. He is not coming to condemn the world, it is already condemned! He is coming to build and establish His kingdom and authority and He will not build it upon the world's foundations. The land must first be cleared of everything which He has not built. "EVERY PLANT WHICH MY HEAVENLY FATHER DID NOT PLANT SHALL BE ROOTED UP," Matt.15:13.

This judgement begins with the household of God for two basic reasons: 1) So that when the world falls apart we will be established in Christ, able to minister life and healing, and 2) because in many areas we need it more than the world does. The church has been very adept at pointing the finger at the world for its sins, while living itself in the same idolatry of self-centeredness, though it did so from behind a cleaner facade.

As stated earlier, an idol is not just something we worship, it is what we trust in and give our attention to. During this time of relative peace and safety many have been lulled into a false security; a security which is not in Christ but in the world and its systems. The Lord is not impressed with religious exercises; one can teach a parrot to do and say the right things. He purchased us with His blood that "we who live should no longer live for ourselves but for Him." Anything less than this is idolatry.

When the rich young ruler wanted to follow Jesus he was required to give up all that he owned. Nothing less would have saved the young man, and nothing less will save us. As the Lord Himself declared: "So therefore, no one of you can be My disciple who does not give up ALL of his own possessions" (LUKE 14:33). In order to make it as easy for people to "make a decision for Christ" we have reduced the gospel until it requires little or nothing from us, and by this we have destroyed its very power to save. These are false gospels which feed the self-centeredness and self-promotion which caused death to enter the world in the beginning, and have been its perpetuating delusion, regardless of whether they are called the gospel or any other philosophy.

Now the day of reckoning is upon us and those for whom the decision was made so easy will soon find this Way intolerably difficult. These will not only fall away in the days to come, they will become some of the most unrelenting enemies of the true gospel. We have done no one a favor by reducing the cost of discipleship. Those who thought they could come and still save their (self) lives, will lose them anyway. Only those who have truly lost their lives to find Him will stand the day that is coming.

Spiritual Immorality And Spiritual Abortion

The church has been pointing its finger at the world for its immorality even while she commits spiritual immorality with the world. As James declared: "You adulteresses, do you not know that friendship with the world is hostility toward God? Therefore whoever wishes to be a friend of the world makes himself an ENEMY OF GOD" (JAMES 4:4). We abhor abortions (as we should), but how many spiritual seeds planted in the church by the Lord have been aborted because we didn't want to bother with carrying them to term? How many potentially great and effective men and women of God are now lifeless pew warmers because we snuffed out the vision God had planted in them for ministry?

We have been quick to point our finger at the world for its abortions while we commit spiritual abortion for the same reasons they commit theirs: it is too inconvenient to carry the spiritual seeds the Lord plants in us to term, we are selfish, or we do not think we can afford them. How many of God's seeds have we aborted before they were born because we could not afford to send them out, while at the same time we gloat over our new multi-million dollar buildings and family life centers. The Lord does hate abortion, and it will bring His wrath, but He is going to start with His own house. If the church were walking in the light that she has the world would not be living in the darkness that it is. We flail at the world's branches but the Lord is about to put the ax to the root of our own tree. The church is supposed to confront the world with its iniquity, but not before we have been examined by the same finger. Only then will we be able to effectively confront the world and its problems. As the apostle explained, "And we are ready to punish all disobedience, WHENEVER YOUR OBEDIENCE IS COMPLETE" (II COR. 10:6).

The church in the West has been like Jonah in the ship. It was Jonah's rebellion that brought the storm upon the heathen in the ship, and it is the church's rebellion that is bringing much of the turmoil upon the world. The heathen in Jonah's story were actually more in touch with reality than was the man of God; they were trying to find God, while the prophet slept! The heathen had to wake up the prophet so he could call on his God. Likewise, many of the heathen in the west have been more discerning of the false gospels and corruption in ministries than the church has been. As the apostle asked the Corinthians, "Do we not judge those who are in the church?" God's love is not the "sloppy agape" we have pretended it to be. When we give approval to the things which God disapproves it is unsanctified mercy and it will bring judgment upon the whole house.

This is not to imply that the world will not also be judged for its evil. It will be judged, but not until we have. As someone well said, "Having a ship in the sea is fine, but when the sea gets in the ship we have a problem!" The church has not impacted the world as much as the world has influenced the church.

When Jesus walked on the earth Israel was certainly the most moral and upstanding nation in existance. The Jews were a very religious people. As is obvious in the gospels, they stoned those who were caught in adultery; they did not tolerate such sin in their midst. Yet the Lord said that it would be more tolerable for Sodom and Gomorrah in the day of judgment than for them! Sodom and Gomorrah were two of the most wicked cities that have ever existed, even by today's standards, yet the Jews, who were so moral and conservative are going to be worse off than they! Why? Because with greater light comes greater accountability. We may measure ourselves by the world and think that we rate pretty good, but God does not look at us like that; He looks at how much light He has given us. Using the standards He gave to the cities of Israel, how is He going to measure us?

A fire is soon to come upon the church which will remove the wood, hay and stubble. Of the works that were done in the Lord's name, but were not by His commission, or of those who have compromised their calling, not one stone will be left upon another. EVERYTHING THAT CAN BE SHAKEN, WILL BE SHAKEN. That which is His will be purified, and will become a glorious scepter in His hand. There is not a church, a ministry, a minister, or an individual, who will not be touched by this fire. We will ALL be humbled, before the Lord, before each other, and before the world. Pride and presumption started the fall, and its removal from the church will end her fall. This is necessary because the greatest exaltation of the church in history is to follow this judgement.

By the Lord's mercy He is going to send a clear word of warning to His people that we might judge ourselves before He has to judge us. He is going to have a holy people. When His wrath does come it will be unrelenting. Let us not presume that ignorance will be acceptable. Everyone will have a chance to hear His warning, but not all will. Many will have been so caught up in their own affairs or distractions they will not have taken the time to listen. Their judgment will be just. There will be no excuse for anyone. Now is the time for us to repent of our lukewarmness and self-seeking, regardless of how we got that way. Let us not keep pointing at the darkness the world is living in if our own light is not shining for them. Let us now return to our first love and our first commitment and never let them be stolen from us again.

The seven churches in Revelation were a prophetic parallel of the entire church age. Beginning with Ephesus, which portrayed the first century church, we can see a remarkable outline of church history. Laodicea, being the last of the seven churches, is a type of the last day church. We usually think of Laodicea as the lukewarm church, and that is indeed our primary problem. We think that we are wealthy, and we are in both material and spiritual blessings, but in life and power we are poor and blind and naked. Even though the Laodicean church received such a devastating verdict of its condition, THE GREATEST PROMISES GIVEN TO ANY CHURCH WERE GIVEN TO LAODICEA, IF SHE REPENTED.

In REV.3:20 we see the Lord knocking at the door of the Laodicean church seeking to personally come in and dine with her. The Lord is waiting to personally give this church more revelation and truth than at any other time in history. Not only do we have the Bible compiled, but we have more copies in circulation today than there were for all of the other church ages combined. We have books, tapes, videos, T.V., and have been blessed with some of the most extraordinary teachers in church history. A man of God can spend his entire life acquiring knowledge and put it in a book which we can absorb in a few hours. Every other seeker of God in history would love to have had what He has given to us, and we have been most lukewarm in our appreciation and use of it. The time has come to arise from our stupor, open the door and let Him in.

What does it means to dine "with Jesus?" After His resurrection even His most intimate disciples had trouble recognizing Him. It is because they were more dependent upon their knowledge of His physical appearance than His heart; they knew Him after the flesh and not after the Spirit. After joining two of His disciples on the road to Emmaus, even when He opened the scriptures to them, they did not recognize Him. It was not until they saw Him <u>breaking the bread</u> that their eyes were opened. The same is true with us. It is when we see Jesus breaking our bread to feed us, not our pastor, not our favorite author, teacher, or televangelist, but the Lord Himself, that our eyes are opened.

It is not just hearing the words of the Lord that matters, but hearing the Word Himself. This is the promise to Laodicea, the last day church: if we hear HIM knocking and open we will dine WITH HIM. Hasn't this been the desire of our hearts from the beginning: not just to know about Him, but to know Him? He is our first love and we will return to Him. This is how the light, the glory and the power to accomplish the last day ministry will come.

In the sons of Jacob, who were to become the twelve tribes of Israel, and in the prophecies spoken over them by Jacob and Moses, there is another prophetic unfolding of church history. The church is spiritual Israel, and the history of the nation of Israel was a prophetic outline of the church's destiny; the natural first and then the spiritual. We can see in Reuben, the firstborn of Jacob, an accurate portrayal of the early church, with the birth of the following sons and the histories of the tribes derived from them as a remarkable picture of church history right down to Benjamin, the last son born and a type of the last day church.

Benjamin was one of three men in scripture born in Bethlehem, the other two being David and Jesus. Bethlehem means "house of bread," or "a place of food," which again reflects the fact that the last day church would be born in the place of abundant spiritual food. When Benjamin and his brothers were invited to eat with Joseph in Egypt, before he had revealed his identity to them, the Scripture says, "And he (Joseph) took portions to them from his own table; BUT BENJAMIN'S PORTION WAS FIVE TIMES AS MUCH AS ANY OF THEIRS..." (GEN.43:44). This was another prophetic incident foretelling the abundant spiritual food to be provided for the last day church.

This abundance of spiritual food in this day exceeds all that of the other church ages and we must take advantage of this great opportunity. The knowledge, understanding, and the outpouring of direct revelation from the Lord is given to us for a reason. We are going to need every bit of it to accomplish the mandate given to us in this hour. It is time to buy from Him the gold that has been refined by fire, those treasures of wisdom and knowledge that have been proven. It is time to buy from Him the garments of purity that will cover our sin and nakedness. And it is time to buy from Him the eyesalve to open our eyes so that we can see from His perspective.

In REV.7:9, we see the great company clothed in white robes who stand BEFORE the throne. To the overcomers of the Laodicean church He promises that they will sit with Him ON His throne. He has made available to this church a position of authority and power that is unprecedented. This is not because of our righteousness, as obviously we have in fact been lukewarm and indifferent during the times of greatest opportunity. This authority He is about to give is being given for one reason: it has never been needed before like it is now. Those who overcome the spirit of lukewarmness will soon do exploits unequaled in Old or New Testament times. The Lord has saved His best wine for last, and those who are zealous for Him are already beginning to partake of it. The glory of the latter house will be greater than the former (HAG.2:9). This does not mean that the latter house was greater, but the glory within it is greater.

We see this promise to the Laodicean overcomer again reflected in the life of Benjamin. When Benjamin was born his mother died. Before she expired she named him Benoni, which means "son of my sorrows." Jacob changed his name to Benjamin, which means "son of my right hand." He was transformed or "raised" from a son of sorrows to his mother, to the son of his father's right hand. The right hand is the position of authority, as Jesus is seated at the right hand of the Father. That the last son was to be named Benjamin was a testimony of the authority with which the last day ministry would come forth.

Benjamin was the only one of the twelve who was named by his father and not his mother. This is a reason for the authority given to this last day ministry: they will not be named, or commissioned, by their mother, the church, but by the Father. Their offices and ministries will not come because of the courses taken in seminary, they will not be dictated by the pressing needs of the church or the people; they will receive their mandate from above. There are men and women alive today who have refused to receive their names from the mother but are patiently waiting to hear the Father's voice say, "This is My beloved Son as a teacher in you" (or apostle, prophet, etc..).

The failure to wait for the Father's commission has resulted in much of the disorientation and spiritual burnout which has caused the lukewarm condition of the present church. It has caused potentially great evangelists to waste their lives trying to be pastors, or teachers trying to be evangelists, etc... Others failed in ministry even though they knew their proper calling, but they mistook the CALLING for the COMMISSIONING. Paul was called as an apostle many years before he was commissioned by the Holy Spirit. The time between the calling and the commissioning is crucial for proper preparation. As Paul explained, "When He who had set me apart from my mother's womb, and CALLED me through His grace, was pleased to reveal His Son IN me (not just TO him), that I might preach..." (GAL.1:15-16). Preparation is not just learning more about Him, or even His ways; it is having Him brought forth IN us.

Miracles were performed by the Lord, not just to confirm His word, but also to BE a message. The first miracle He performed is one of the most important for us to understand. By His first miracle He was illustrating to the disciples He had just called what was the initial work to be done in them. He had the vessels set aside, which were typical of the disciples, and He had them filled to the brim with water. The water is typical of His word (see EPH.5:26) with which He was going to fill them. He then turned the water into wine, symbolizing that He would turn His word into Spirit and Life in them.

Anyone may teach about God's love, but only those who have laid down their lives with Him can impart that love. Anyone can teach truths, but only those who have given their lives in search of it can impart a love for the truth, which is the essence of the true teaching ministry. The knowledge and ability to impart facts can easily be attained through study and practice; the apostolic ability to impart life can only be attained by taking up our crosses daily, following Him, and like Him, doing all things for the sake of the gospel.

For the last day ministry the Lord has set aside a number

47

of "vessels" who have patiently waited for their water to be turned into wine. These are about to be released with such life and power in their message that the church will be just as stunned as the headwaiter was at the wedding in Cana. The Lord has again saved His best wine for last. After we have tasted it we will never again be content with the lifeless water of mere formulas and principles, contrived by the minds of those who substitute mental gymnastics for the ways of the Spirit.

Laodicea was exhorted to "be ZEALOUS therefore and repent," because a lack of zeal was the root of her problem. We must recognize the reasons for our lukewarmness if we are to be delivered from it. As stated, one significant cause is the present religious system. It has put its own yokes on those trying to serve the Lord, forcing them into positions because of the needs of the church instead of the calling to a particular ministry. The present system has become more responsive to the people's yokes than to the Lord's yoke. His is the only yoke that we are to carry. When we find the courage to resist the pressures of the people to do only that which the Lord has called us to, we will have far more of that which is true life to give the people than we do now. Our tendency to carry the yokes of the people in place of the Lord's is certainly the number one cause of burnout in ministry today.

Another reason for the lukewarmness of Laodicea is found in Jeremiah 50:6:

My people have become lost sheep; their shepherds have led them astray. They have made them turn aside on the mountains; they have gone along from mountain to hill and have forgotten their resting place.

Going from mountain to hill speaks of going from one thing that stimulates to the next, hype to hype; keeping the people excited, but never leading them to the resting place, the Lord of the Sabbath. This compulsion to keep people stimulated and moving is rooted in the insecurity of the Saul nature, being afraid that if we allow the level of excitement to drop the people will start scattering from us. But the church is weary of projects and hype, and she now wants the Lord, as the preceeding verses in Jeremiah explain:

> In those days and at that time," declares the Lord, "the sons of Israel will come, both they and the sons of Judah as well; they will go along weeping as they go, and IT WILL BE THE LORD THEIR GOD THEY WILL SEEK. They will ask for the way to Zion, turning their faces in its direction; THEY WILL COME THAT THEY MAY JOIN THEMSELVES TO THE LORD in an everlasting covenant that will not be forgotten (JER.50:4-5).

Megaministries, projects and organizations will never again receive the kind of support that they have in the past. Most of the church has finally wised up to the hype and condemnation tactics used to solicit their support. The church will not continue to be distracted by the "cities" which men build, she is now starting to look for the one built by God. The laborers about to be sent by the Lord will not just be builders of projects and ministries, they will build people; making "living stones" into a habitation for our God, that He might dwell among us.

The meaning of the name Laodicea reflects another reason for the lukewarmness now afflicting much of the church. Laodicia means "judging by the people." This speaks first of the critical, judgemental spirit which results in our separation from God and each other. Isaiah 58:9 says, "Then you will call, and the Lord will answer; you will cry and He will say, 'Here I am,' IF YOU REMOVE THE YOKE FROM YOUR MIDST, THE POINTING OF THE FINGER AND SPEAKING WICKEDNESS."

When we are critical of the Lord's people we are in fact being critical of the Lord Himself. By this we are really saying that the Lord's work in this person's life does not meet our standards. This is a grievous error that leads to a terrible darkness of soul. Inevitably, the things of which we are the most critical in others are our own worst problems. By such judgement we keep ourselves and others in bondage.

Much of this is rooted in the power of the "two thieves" discussed earlier. We tend to keep others, and ourselves, in bondage to yesterday. The Lord is moving in and changing

49

everyone who seeks Him. When we continue to relate to each other according to how we were, instead of giving each other the grace to be that new creature God has made us, we are making it more difficult for everyone to walk in the grace of God and their true callings. This is a yoke that has resulted in much weariness, therefore lukewarmness, in this church age.

Another aspect of this "judging by the people" is the democratic spirit prevalent in the church. Because fallen men have the tendency to be corrupted by power, democracy has proven to be the safest form of government for human affairs. Carried over into the church it can be devastating and misleading. The kingdom of God is just that, a KINGDOM. Our king must be Lord of all, or He will not be our Lord at all. Rule by committee or popular consensus has sent a great part of confessing Christendom down the deadly path to humanism.

A man once keenly observed, "Well if the Lord doesn't show up tonight we've got a pretty good program anyway!" Is that not what has happened? Unable to wait patiently for the Lord (which He always requires), we have determined to get something going to keep the people interested. Is this not what caused Aaron to make the golden calf? The people could not wait for Moses to come down from the mountain and they had to have something to get them going again. How many weak leaders, like Aaron, have given way to this pressure. How many golden calves, symbolic of carnal strength, have been served in our sanctuaries? An idol is not just a graven image, but it is anything that the people trust in place of the one true God. Like Moses did with the golden calf, the time has come when the Lord is going to grind all of our substitutes for Him into powder.

CHAPTER 4

KINGDOM AUTHORITY

When the people came to make Jesus king He fled to the mountains. We may consider this a noble intention on the part of the people, but it was in fact one of the most presumptuous acts recorded in scripture. Mere men thought that they could make God king! If the people make you king who rules? The people. Jesus could not be made king; He was BORN king.

The same is true of spiritual ministry. If it is the people who we derive our authority from they will be the ones who rule, not God. This is a primary reason for the church's lack of power and authority. We have been taking men's yokes instead of the Lord's. One only has true spiritual authority to the degree that the King reigns within them.

Before the church can walk in true prophetic authority it must take the position that Elijah did. When he first appeared to King Ahab his statement was, "As the Lord, the God of Israel lives, BEFORE WHOM I STAND..." (I Kings 17:1). Elijah's statement revealed that he was not standing before Ahab; he was just a man; it was the Lord who lives before Whom Elijah was standing. It was the Lord, not men, before Whom he lived his life. That was the source of Elijah's authority and power, and it is the source of ours. If we are living our lives before the thrones of men we will be false prophets. Elijah knew better than to confuse God's approval with man's. The church has tended to confuse being a witness to the resurrection of Jesus with being acceptable to men. This is one of the most corrupting delusions afflicting the church. When defending his apostleship, the first fact which Paul directed attention to was: "Am I not free?" (I COR.9:1).

Of what is an apostle required to be free? In another statement Paul claimed to be a slave of Christ. It is precisely by this slavery to Christ that we are freed to be sent by Him. As Isaiah stated: "It is the Lord of hosts whom you should regard as holy. And He shall be your fear, and He shall be

51

your dread, THEN He shall become a sanctuary" (IS.8:13-14). If we have the true and holy fear of the Lord we will not fear anything else. Then He becomes our sanctuary! Then our work will be untainted by human motives and self-promotion.

The apostolic commission of Paul was destined to arouse the rage and opposition, not only of the religious establishment, but of the entire Roman Empire. This frail earthen vessel charged unrelentingly into the face of the most powerful principalities and powers of his age, without compromise or consideration for his own life. When the Roman officials exclaimed that Paul was turning the world upside down it was an accurate comprehension of the power of apostolic preaching. This preaching shakes the powers in heaven and earth, and it will solicit their most vehement wrath. Freedom from the fear of man and demon is a prerequisite for a true ministry. As Paul explained to the Galatians: "For am I now seeking the favor of men, or of God? Or am I striving to please men? IF I WERE STILL TRYING TO PLEASE MEN, I WOULD NOT BE A BOND-SERVANT OF CHRIST (GAL.1:10).

Jesus declared, "You are those who justify yourselves in the sight of men, but God knows your hearts; for that which is highly esteemed among men is detestable in the sight of God" (LUKE 16:15). We have a choice to make; if we want to do that which is esteemed by men we are going to be doing that which is detestable to God. The degree to which we seek to please and gain the acceptance of men is the degree to which our message will be diluted, and it will be detestable in our Lord's eyes, regardless of how piously we may use His name. As Jesus exhorted: "Woe to you when all men speak well of you, for in the same way their fathers used to treat the false prophets!" (LUKE 6:26).

To preach an apostolic message it has to be settled in our heart whose approval we are seeking, God or man's. As Jesus asked His disciples, "How can you believe, when you receive glory from one another, and do not seek the glory that is from the one and only God?" (JOHN 5:44). The compulsion to have the acceptance of men erodes our faith as well as the message. It was for this reason that Paul had to rebuke the first apostle to preach the resurrection of Jesus, Peter, "because he stood condemned." (GAL.2:11-14). Peter had compromised the straightforwardness of the gospel because he feared the Jewish believers. This same tendency had previously resulted in Peter getting called "Satan" by Jesus because he was setting his mind on man's interests instead of God's (see MATT.16:21-23).

Spiritual authority demands freedom from the fear of man, but this freedom must be salted with the wisdom to avoid being unnecessarily offensive. This is what Paul meant when he said, "For though I am free from all men, I have made myself a slave to all, THAT I MIGHT WIN THE MORE. To the Jews I became as a Jew, THAT I MIGHT WIN JEWS... (I COR.9:19-20). Paul adjusted his lifestyle somewhat to the customs of those he was trying to reach, not because he feared them or wanted their approval, but because he loved them and wanted to save them.

The Mount Of Transfiguration

The second fact which Paul used to establish his authority was "Have I not seen the Lord?" This is another of the primary prerequisites for true spiritual authority. We must challenge ourselves with this same question. Who are we seeing, Ahab or the living God?

The Mount of Transfiguration is a good example of why our vision must be concentrated on Jesus and not men. Jesus took Peter, James and John up to a high mountain (see MATT.17:1-8). Jesus was transfigured and Moses and Elijah appeared talking to Him. This was a testimony that the ministries of Moses (the law) and Elijah (the prophets) were to speak of Him. Upon seeing this great revelation it says, "And Peter ANSWERED." Nobody was talking to Peter! This is what usually gets us into the same trouble Peter often found himself in; we start talking and making plans before we even understand what the revelation means. Peter's reaction was a common human response to a great spiritual revelation: "Lord, it is good for us to be here, I WILL...." (v.4). Peter's good intention was in fact an echo of Satan himself personified in Isaiah 14: "I WILL ascend to heaven. I WILL raise my throne, I WILL...

The good of the Tree of Knowledge is just as deadly as the evil because they are both from the same root. As Paul explained to the men of Athens, "Human hands cannot serve Him (ACTS 17:25). History is littered with the refuse of great spiritual revelations that, instead of shaking and challenging the kingdoms of this world, went on to be absorbed by them, actually increasing the dominion of Babylon instead of the Kingdom of God.

It was good for Peter to be on that mountain, but not for the reasons that arose in his heart. It was good for him to hear the rebuke of the Father, "This is My beloved Son, HEAR HIM!" It was good for Peter to have the fear of God overshadow him after his great presumption. This was all good because after this it says of the three, "And lifting up their eyes, they saw no one, EXCEPT JESUS HIMSELF, ALONE" (v.8). Jesus ALONE must be the vision of those who would be apostolic.

The glory of the Lord is soon to be revealed to His people, and then upon them. In some cases this will be an actual visible manifestation. His presence will be known until His nearness is the consuming desire of our hearts. As He draws near to us there will be almost no attention or concern given to the temples we've made, the works, projects, the campaigns and hype which have so wearied and burdened the church and have been a primary cause for the prevailing luke-warmness.

After the resurrection of Jesus, Peter and some of the disciples decided to go fishing. They labored all night and caught nothing. The next morning the Lord appeared on the bank and told them to cast their nets on the other side. Immediately their nets were full. Peter, realizing that it was the Lord, jumped into the sea and swam ashore. After spending just a few minutes in the presence of Jesus, Peter then went down and by himself drew in the net with which all of the other disciples had been fiercely struggling. A few minutes in His presence will empower us to accomplish far more than multiplied human effort.

Good is the worst enemy of best. There is a gospel, a church, a ministry and a religion which calls itself Christian, but compels us to feel safe in a spiritual condition in which we remain lost and void of life. If the pursuit of happiness and comfort is our primary motivation we will forever be fooled. If we are to respond to our callings and walk in truth a commitment to the reality of ROM. 12:1 will be required-- that we present ourselves as a living and holy sacrifice. A choice is now being presented to us; we can pay now or pay later. To walk in the truth of the gospel will cost us every- thing now; to not walk in it will cost us everything later.

Babylon

As a wise man once observed, "Those who forget history are doomed to repeat it." EVERY new move of God has event- ually fallen to the same errors made by each previous move. The lack of a historical perspective in the church has resulted in her repeating the same devastating mistakes over and over. The Lord is about to break this cycle, but we must under- stand it to be delivered. In chapters 17 & 18 of Revelation we have an illumination of "Mystery Babylon." This system is the fruit of the same error being perpetuated for generation after generation in the church. To properly understand this mystery we must go to its root--the Tower of Babel.

The building of the tower of Babel is a lucid revelation of the delusions of religious selfish ambition. This is one of the great manifestations of the same lie started in the garden; that we can be like God without God. The men of Shinar thought they could make it to heaven by their own might and power, building a tower. We may ridicule these men, but the church has continually tried to do the same thing. Building the tower "to heaven" was just a guise for their real motive, which they clearly expressed:

Come LET US BUILD FOR OURSELVES a city and a tower whose top will reach into heaven, and LET US MAKE A NAME FOR OURSELVES; lest we be scattered abroad over the face of the whole earth (GEN.11:4).

After Christianity became the state religion in the third

century, politics replaced worship and sacrifice in the ministry. With this change the motives of building for ourselves, and making names for ourselves, entered and gradually took over as the true vision of the church. Men thought that they could establish the kingdom of God on earth with the sword, crusades, inquisitions and tortures. It is estimated by historians that over fifty million "heretics," who were in fact true believers who refused to submit to this error, were killed by this beast. She was drunk with the blood of the saints and the true witnesses of Jesus (REV. 17:6). For over 1,200 years she ruled over the kings of the earth. She did not take temporal authority, but no one else could without her consent. The Lord looked down upon this abomination and prescribed the same remedy that He did for the first tower--He scattered their languages. Now we have over 20,000 different languages, or denominations.

Everything we have built that was really for us, or to make a name for ourselves, is a part of this evil which is about to be destroyed. The call in REV.18:4 is now going forth, "Come out of her My people, that you may not participate in her sins and that you may not receive of her plagues." But He has not called us to come out without leading us to something greater. Just as there is a clear revelation of the Mystery Babylon sweeping the body of Christ, there is also a clear revelation of the City Of God being imparted.

It will not benefit us to come out of physical Babylon if the spirit of that system remains in our hearts. Coming out of Babylon means far more than leaving a denomination. There are some "nondenominational" churches which are more sectarian than many denominational churches. Likewise, there are some denominational churches which seem to have little or no sectarian spirit. We can put "non-denominational" on our signs and statements of faith, refuse all extra-local organizations, and do everything else which contrasts that system, but if we are still building for ourselves and seeking a reputation we are still a part of that system and destined to be doomed with it.

This is not just a matter of having correct doctrines, but deliverance from a heart condition. As Thomas A'Kempis reflected, "What good does it avail a man to be able to discourse profoundly concerning the Trinity, if he is void of humility and thereby displeasing to the Trinity?" Leaving Babylon is laying down our self-seeking and the divisions which separate us from the Lord and each other. Just because one complies with correct doctrines does not mean this has been accomplished. For this reason Paul explained, "From now on we recognize no man (or church) according to the flesh (externals), but according to the spirit."

Babylon means "confusion" because it was there that God confused men's languages. James explained, "For where jealousy and selfish ambition exist, there is DISORDER (confusion, "Babylon") and EVERY EVIL THING" (JAMES 3:16). It does not matter how piously we attach the Lord's name to our works, every work that is motivated by selfish ambition is about to suffer the judgement prophesied by John in The Revelation. Because He has tolerated this spirit for so long we too have tolerated presumption and self-seeking with hardly a question, sometimes even encouraging it. That day is now at an end. If we continue in that system, we will partake of her sins, and we will receive of her plagues.

This is not to imply that just because we have good intentions when trying to build something for God that it is His work. As previously stated, the "good" of the Tree of Knowledge is just as deadly as the evil; their root is the same. Ministry which is motivated by an attempt to gain God's approval is just as much an affront to Him. Jesus paid the price for our acceptance. Anything additionally offered by us to gain God's acceptance is a statement that we don't believe His sacrifice was good enough to accomplish this. True ministry can only come from a position of HAVING God's approval, not trying to acquire it. When Jesus said "It is finished" He was declaring that there was nothing left to be done. JESUS IS the Alpha and Omega, the Beginning and the End of the work of God. We cannot take anything away from, or add anything to, what He has already accomplished.

This does not mean that because the work is finished we are not to build anything, but the difference is in HOW we build. As the apostle explained:

For no man can lay a foundation other than the One

57

which is laid, which IS JESUS CHRIST. Now if any man builds upon the foundation with gold, silver, precious stones, wood, hay, straw, each man's work will become evident; FOR THE DAY WILL SHOW IT, because it is to be revealed with fire; and the fire itself will test the quality of each man's work (I COR.3:11-13).

Jesus is the foundation, and in a true sense, He is also the entire building--"All things are to be summed up in Him." He is the Alpha, the foundation, and he is also the Omega, the Capstone. This was the apostolic message. Almost everything being called "apostolic" today emphasizes form, but the true apostolic message gave no emphasis to form. They did things to help bring and keep order, like appointing elders, etc.., but their emphasis was not on form, but formation. They labored that Christ would be formed IN the church, not that the church would come into a certain form. This emphasis on form instead of spirit has been the bane and ultimate doom of every move of God since the apostolic age, and will continue to be until that which is apostolic is raised up again.

Even some of the ministries being raised up to ignite the coming move of God will have this tendency to think that if they have the right form for the church it will hold together. This is the same deception motivating the men of Shinar; believing that their new formula or project could keep men from being scattered. ONLY "In Him (do) all things hold together" (COL.1:17). Some who will be mightily used of God in the next move will crash on the same rocks as did the previous movements if this is not understood. Even so, out of this next move there will come those who have a vision for that which is truly apostolic. These will have been delivered from the Babylonian spirit, not just the Babylonian forms, and they will be used to give birth to that which is the true faith of the fathers, the forming of Jesus within. It is "Christ in us the hope of Glory."

Every Restoration move until now has been reduced to emphasizing doctrine and form. The apostolic faith will emphasize Life, Himself. Until now we have been content to have the Lord revealed TO us, but a day is coming when He will be revealed IN us. We only need new wineskins IF we have new wine. It is a devastating delusion for us to think that merely having a new wineskin can produce the new wine.

In the Book of Revelation we see that one can see Babylon from the valley, but we must be taken to a "high mountain" to see the New Jerusalem. One is not delivered from the Babylonian spirit just by seeing it, or even understanding it. History testifies that many who clearly see and understand this beast are consumed by the same spirit because they do not have a vision of the New Jerusalem. Many of those who preach vehemently against Babylon do so out of the same sectarian spirit. Their preaching inevitably results in a perpetuation of the same Babylonian confusion: more sects who think they alone are right.

We are changed by what we are beholding (II COR.3:18). If Babylon has all of our attention it will consume us. If we are beholding the glory of the Lord we will be changed into that same light, which will itself expose that which is darkness. The destruction of Babylon and her ruler will come "without human agency" (DAN.8:25). As we enter and live in the City of God, judgement on Babylon will be automatic.

When the first two disciples began to follow Jesus, He challenged them with a question that sooner or later we must all answer: "What do you seek?" Their reply was another question, but it was a most appropriate one. "Lord, where do you dwell?" They did not ask which sect was the most scriptural or doctrinally correct, but where did the Lord Himself dwell. This is the only way we can discern the works which are ordained by Him from those that are not.

We must distinguish between the things which God blesses and those which He inhabits. Ishmael was a work of the flesh, was born of the bondwoman and remains in bondage (GAL.4: 21-31). Ishmael was not the promised seed, but persecuted the true heir, and does so to this day, yet, God blessed him and made him a great nation! He blessed him because of the covenant He had with Abraham, and He often blesses our works of the flesh, to a degree, because of the covenant He has made with us: BUT HE WILL NOT INHABIT THEM. A time will come when the child of the flesh must be cast out. We must now look beyond that which may have a blessing upon it and give our attention to that which He inhabits.

Ishmael could remain in the house of Abraham until he began to mock and persecute Issac. This is the separation point which begins to distinguish the works that originate in the flesh and those who are born of the promise; those who are born of the flesh will sooner or later not be able to resist attacking the works which they feel have encroached on their territory. Issac did not have to attack Ishmael because he knew who he was and was not threatened by Ishmael. The works of the flesh are not so secure. These will often do their attacking under the veil of being protectors of the truth, watchmen for the church, etc., but the true motivation is always territorial preservation.

Strong Delusions

For nearly 2,000 years the Lord has been working to prepare His church for this hour. Satan has been earnestly working to deceive, if he could, even the elect who were called from the beginning to serve in this day. One of his most effective delusions has been to get us to devote our attention to who we are in Christ, instead of who He is in us. This usually leads to the worshiping of ourselves, the creature, instead of the blessed Creator.

Regardless of our pretense, we are worshipping that which has our attention. Satan knows we will never become "who we are in Christ" as long as that is our motivation. We will only become who we are called to be when Jesus and His glory are the concentration of our attention. We will only be changed by seeing His glory, not our own (as if we had any of our own). The delusion of getting us to focus on who we are instead of who He is, has side-tracked and led into extremes many of the truths restored in preparation for this hour. But this delusion will not prevail; the glory of the Lord is about to dispel it like a wisp of smoke before a great wind.

Indeed the latter glory of the Lord's house will be greater than the former. This does not mean that the house is greater, but the glory which fills it is greater. When the glory fills the temple it is not the temple that gets your attention. The Lord earnestly testified that those who do attain to all that He has called us to will not even be aware of it; their attention will not be on what they have attained, but on pleasing the One who sent them. The believers who walk in the fullness of what is to come will not be focused on serving the temple of the Lord, but the Lord of the temple. The church, ministry, spiritual truth, even the Bible, can become an idol when it becomes the FOCUS of our attention. Those who overcome and fulfill their callings do so by following the Lamb wherever He goes.

The delusion of self-centeredness and self-worship that now permeates the church, and much of its teaching, will be broken. The Lord Himself is about to enter His temple, and all crowns will be cast at His feet. Those who have presumed to positions of leadership without commission will be evident to all. Everyone who has exalted himself will be humbled. Those who have humbled themselves will be anointed and commissioned. This army now being formed will be greater than anything ever seen or dreamed of, but this army will not be magnifying itself, but the King who leads it.

Those who perform the greatest works will be taking little notice of their own accomplishments. They will not esteem themselves highly, not because of insecurity, but because of their recognition of the One who works through them, and what He has accomplished. These will not be measuring themselves by others, but by Him. Just as the Queen of Sheba was speechless before Solomon's wisdom and the glory of his kingdom, those who have seen Jesus are even far more so before Him. Those who have seen the Lord, like Him, will flee to the mountains when men try to make them kings or exalt them in any way. Their authority will not come through man, it will come from above.

During this harvest human authority and institutions will be melting like wax. As the masses will be seeking anyone to take authority during these times, this comes as a warning! There will be doctrines promulgated encouraging believers to seek authority through institutional and political means. The Lord's kingdom is not of this world and His kingdom will NOT come through this present world's systems. The enemy will use these doctrines to attract those who are self-seeking and self-promoting; the Lord will also use them to separate the tares from the wheat. Those with such motives will not have leadership in this harvest. The authority the Lord will establish is different from what even His own people now perceive. Do not try to rule, just SERVE. Through this His authority will flow and begin to bring order though Peace.

Twentieth century Christianity has become quite adept at converting men from the evil side of the Tree Of Knowledge while not touching the "good" side of the same tree, which is just as deadly and far more deceptive. In Israel, the most evil, and even the demon possessed, bowed the knee to Jesus. It was the most upstanding, citizens who crucified Him. Man's goodness is offered as a compensation for righteousness and is therefore an affront to the cross. It is a statement that we don't think we need the propitiation made for us by Jesus. Man's goodness is as filthy rags in the sight of God, and is a far more formidable enemy to the gospel than the evil side of that tree. It will be those who are eating from the "good" of the Tree of Knowledge who bring the greatest persecution against the advancing church. It will be the "good" fruit from the Tree of Knowledge which deceives and causes more to stumble than the manifest evil of these times.

Some of the ministries who will bring the greatest life to the church in the days to come will be those who have made the worst mistakes in the past. It is a Biblical and historical reality that most fail so totally that they come to the end of all human effort and strength before God will use them. One must be humbled before they can be exalted.

We see this example in Abraham bringing forth Ishmael. Joseph saw the sun and moon and stars bowing to him, but first he had to become a slave, then a prisoner. Moses tried to deliver his brethren by his own strength and had to spend 40 years in the wilderness as a shepherd, the most humble profession of the times, before God could use him. David, after being anointed as the next king, spent years as a fugitive from the very people he was called to rule. Peter had to deny the Lord before he could be used as one of His greatest witnesses. Paul had to become the chief of sinners, persecuting the church unto death, before he could be the "apostle of grace." This may not be true for all, but it seems to be for those who would be the used for the greatest spiritual advances. Many of the elders and fathers of the church would put little trust in anyone who had not been broken by such failure or discipline.

This is not meant to reflect on any individuals as we examine some of the recent mistakes in the body of Christ. As stated above, many of the individuals involved will be more useful to the Lord because of their failures, and we will be losers if we are not open to this. Nevertheless, we must understand the failures or we will be doomed to repeat them. Let us also comprehend that just understanding the problems of the past will not keep us from repeating them. Hearts must be changed by repentance and seeing the Lord's glory more clearly; we must both STOP eating of the Tree of Knowledge and START eating of the Tree of Life. Just doing one without the other will not accomplish our deliverance.

In the 1960's and 70's many great truths were restored to the church. Even though some of these were timely and needed, they were carried to extremes and used to derail a renewal, leading much of the church into stagnation and disorientation. This was not due to any fault in the truths, but in their application. Even correct doctrine, when it becomes an end instead of a means, will be carried to extremes. Then there will be overreactions which usually cause just as much damage as the extremes.

The early church had encounters with God, and then wrote about them. Since then we have been willing to substitute having a correct concept of the truth for the encounter with God. This has resulted in having a form of godliness without God.

For example, how many have studied the community of the early church, duplicated everything they did in order to effect the same spirit and commitment to church life, only to come up with emptiness? The early church did not have community because they did things in a certain way, but because God was moving in their midst. When God is moving all His people want to do is meet; material possessions just do not matter much anymore and we freely give them to one another as unto the Lord. It is God moving that makes truth life. If He is not moving all of our formulas and principles will just cause death.

Christianity is not just a system of truths and principles, it is a relationship with a living God. Truths and principles instituted before the relationship is established are still rooted in the Tree of Knowledge, and regardless of how accurate the truths may be, death will be their ultimate fruit. Only when the relationship is established are we safe to implement truths and principles.

Consider the doctrine of submission to authority. This was a timely truth for the body of Christ. The world and the church were under an onslaught of lawlessness and disorientation. But much of the application of this truth actually brought about fruit that was contrary to the very doctrine itself. Many of the most humble and submissive men and women of God were blackballed from ministry because they did not comply with certain people's doctrine of submission. At the same time, some of the most arrogant and rebellious individuals were released and promoted in the church because they complied with, or believed in, the doctrine. Which is preferable, having a correct doctrine of submission or being submissive? The truth that God requires is not in the minds, but in the hearts. The Lord never said we would know those who were His because they have their doctrines lined up right. There is only one way that we can ever discern those who are true servants, BY THEIR FRUIT.

There have been "lone rangers" causing confusion in the body of Christ, but all of the lone rangers combined hardly caused the confusion of the few who overemphasized submission. Nowhere does the scripture warn us to beware of those who are not submitted to the body; the warning is to beware of those who are not joined to the Head. According to many popular doctrines of submission one can be "properly" joined to the body without even being joined to the Head, and many are. But if one is truly joined to the Head they will be properly joined to the body also, though it may not be in a way that complies with our doctrine, or meets our approval.

The issue is not whether we should be joined to the body properly, but just how this is to be accomplished. The church has displayed a two thousand year old tendency to put the cart in front of the horse. The church is not an end, but a means. The end of all things is to be summed up in Christ.

The whole purpose of God for His people is that they be conformed to the image of His Son. We do not become the church in order to do this; we become the church WHEN we have done this. The church is NOT the pattern for the church; JESUS IS THE PATTERN FOR THE CHURCH. Everytime we get beguiled from this simplicity of devotion to Christ, not the church, not a doctrine, and not even His servants, but devotion to the Lord HIMSELF, we lose our way.

When a major televangelist confessed his sins publicly, he made the statement that he did not really have a single friend that he could be open and share his problems with. This statement was taken by many as THE reason for his problems. Though he had so many people around him, and seemed to have conformed to all of the principles of submission to the body, he was obviously not truly submitted. Even so, his failure to be submitted to the church was not the problem, but just a symptom of a much deeper problem, one that all will face who are so given to majoring on minors.

In some of the counsels of elders and leaders with the very highest standards of mutual accountability and submission, immorality and homosexuality has arisen that had been going on for years. This alone should wake us up to the fact that something was seriously wrong with our concept of submission. The moral, ethical, and heretical problems arising from the church are not because there is not enough submission to the body, but because there is not enough submission to the Head. We can fool our most intimate associates, our families, and even the press, but we cannot fool God. The problems that have been surfacing in the church are because of a lack of the true and holy fear of the Lord. The answer to this is not to throw out our submission to one another, but to give even greater emphasis to that which is even more important, our submission to the Lord. Only then will our submission to each other be real.

The reducing of truth from the Person to a mere doctrine has led to the distortion of every truth restored over the last few centuries. When Martha approached Jesus after the death of her brother, He told her that Lazarus would rise again. She said she knew he would on the last day. Her faith was in the doctrine of the resurrection, not in Him. He redirected her faith, saying, "I am the Resurrection." Jesus is not only the resurrection, he is all truth.

It is possible to have all of our doctrines lined up properly but not have life. It is also possible to have life in Jesus before we have all of our doctrines lined up right. We see a good example of this in Martha and Mary. When Martha declared that had Jesus been there her brother would not have died, she got a real good teaching about the resurrection. When her sister Mary came out and asked the identical question Jesus, "being deeply moved in spirit," He wept, and then He raised Lazarus from the dead. Martha got a good teaching; Mary got results. That's because Mary had a relationship with Jesus that could move Him "deeply in spirit." Even though Mary was just as wrong in her understanding as Martha, Mary could move God Himself deeply; she could cause God Himself to weep. Mary had chosen the "best part."

Jesus is Truth, and those who love Him love truth. We do want our understanding to be accurate, but having our facts right is not as important as our relationship to Him. If our relationship to Him is not right, having all doctrines laid out properly is still eating from the Tree of Knowledge, and it will still bring death.

As a good demonstration of this delusion, we have many of the "faith" teachings being promulgated today. These reduce faith to principles and formulas until it becomes a faith in one's faith in place of faith in God. True faith is simply the recognition of the One in whom we believe. Jesus is not only the Resurrection. He is Faith, and He is every Truth. He is "I AM." That's why Paul declared, 'For as many as may be the promises of God, IN HIM they are yes" (II COR.1:20). He further testified of this to the Galatians: "Now the promises were spoken to Abraham and to his seed. He does not say, 'and to his seeds,' as referring to many, BUT RATHER TO ONE, 'and to your Seed,' THAT IS CHRIST'" (GAL.3:16). The promises of God are not given to us independently of Him, but IN Him. The promises were not given to be consumed by our selfish desires, they were given for His glory. To get us to use the promises of God for selfish reasons has been one of Satan's most effective temptations; so successful he even tried to use it on Jesus.

Some have carried these doctrines to an even more dangerous extreme; presuming to use God's authority ON HIM! This is what cost Moses his inheritance in the promised land. He was told once to strike the Rock, which was a type of Christ Who was to be struck ONCE (see I COR. 10:4). The next time he was to bring water from the Rock he was directed to "speak to the Rock." This was to symbolize that once Christ was struck all we would have to do was to speak to Him and the living waters would flow. But Moses allowed his frustration with the people to drive him to strike the Rock again, using the rod that God had given him. The rod speaks of the authority God does give to us, but we are not to use it to strike Him with it. Such presumption can likewise cost us our inheritance.

Every truth will be carried to extremes by some. Others, because of the extremes, reject the truth altogether. Both have missed God. Those who carry truth to extremes are usually corrected and learn valuable lessons from their mistakes. Those who sit in judgment and fear of error often become like the dwarfs in C.S. Lewis' The Last Battle. When the battle was over and Aslan, who was the Christ figure, came to let them out of their dreary hiding place, they refused to come out! They were sure that He was just another deceiver and they could not be delivered from their darkness. Those who are the most fearful of error are the most difficult to lead out into light, and usually spend their lives in a most dreary place. The fear of deception will not keep us from deception; it will lead to our deception. The ONLY thing which will keep us from being deceived is a love for the Truth, Himself.

No one wants to make mistakes. It would be a horrible thing to be responsible for allowing injury to a neighbor's child. How much more grievous is it to cause one of the Lord's children to stumble? As James warned us, teaching is a serious matter: "Let not many of you become teachers, my brethren, knowing that as such we shall incur a stricter judgment" (JAMES 3:1). The worst thing in scripture that one can be is a stumbling block. The judgment soon to come upon the household of God will be even more intense upon the teachers. If we are wise teachers we will pray for it. His judgment is for our salvation, not condemnation. It is better to receive the discipline of the Lord than to lead even one of His little ones astray.

After the judgement of His household there will not be as many teachers. Teaching in His name will be seen as the holy and serious matter that it is. The teachers who are left will not be given to the elaboration of mere facts and principles, but to the impartation of a love for the Truth. As the old proverb explained, "If you give a man a fish he has one meal. If you teach him how to fish he can feed himself for the rest of his life." Those who are taught about God are never filled. Those who are taught to love God will soon have a river of living water flowing out of their own innermost being.

Saul Comes Before David

With almost everything the Lord does there is a "Saul" before there is a "David." That is, there will be man's choice for the provision before God's. This includes ministries, movements and restored truths. When we see what takes place with truths like submission, discipleship, faith and others, we need to understand that this is because God is about to speak concerning these areas. There is a degree of submission He will require in the days to come which exceeds the present comprehension of this for most of the church. There is a true discipleship that we need in this hour like never before. There is to be a faith required in the days to come which greatly exceeds that which we presently know.

We must understand that Saul was anointed by God and he did accomplish some of the purposes of God. Many of Saul's devoted followers did recognize David in time and joined his company as honored leaders. Many who may have been in the service of what could be recognized as "Saul", were men of faith and courage who pushed beyond the present limits of faith. Their work may have been sidetracked, but it has helped prepare the way for that which we might call "David."

The men of Israel started to feel their need for a king because the Lord had put that need in their hearts. He was preparing them for the king He had promised, whose lineage would be from the tribe of Judah and who would reign until Shiloh (Jesus) came (GEN.49:10). Samuel was raised up as a prophet to prepare Israel for this king and to anoint him (as a type of John the Baptist). But Israel could not wait for God's king, just as Abraham could not wait for Issac. Saul was man's king, not God's. God's king was not yet mature enough to take his place. In the same way we can get sidetracked with present truth. We see the truth, we know it's needed, so we move out to establish it before it is the FULLNESS of time.

Israel's impatience cost them. After Saul it took them a long time to accept God's true king. So it is with almost every truth the Lord restores to the church. Seldom have men been able to wait for God's provision before they went on to formulate that which is merely human strivings. Man's provision must always die before God's provision can take its place. Even though that which is God's provision may move to Hebron and be accepted by some, it usually takes a good while for the rest of the church to receive it. This cycle is prevalent throughout church history.

Even in the days of Saul's reign there were some who recognised David as the Lord's king. These joined him in the cave of obscurity and humility. Just as David was prepared for his calling and authority by his rejection, humiliation and tribulations, so the truths of God are purified in those who receive them, but hold to them, in spite of the fire's testing.

Those who joined themselves to David in the cave were misfits in Israel, and so are those who are usually the first to recieve God's truths. But the caves transformed them along with David; they became some of the greatest warriors and most faithful leaders in Israel's history. The great truths which have transformed the church and changed the course of history have seldom come out of the ivory towers of esoteric theological discourse. The vessels of prophetic truth have almost always been the obscure spiritual misfits who live in spiritual caves and holes in the ground. So it is to be in the coming days.

We need not be discouraged by the doctrines which seem to just rip and confuse the body of Christ. When the doctrines of men rise to create such havoc, we can take courage that

God's truth in the matter has already been born and will mature until the proper time for its revelation. The different "Sauls" will just help us to appreciate the "Davids" that much more. There is true revelation from God coming on faith, discipleship, spiritual authority, the kingdom, unity, as well as many other doctrines which may now be confusing the body of Christ. Do not be misled by any new teaching which seems to be head and shoulders above the rest. When such a doctrine arises, start looking for the young shepherds faithfully tending their little flocks, or the little bands of misfits hiding in caves. That is where we will find the truth until Saul is dead.

Saul was anointed as king by the Lord. As stated, because of God's covenant with Israel (and the church), He will bless our seed, even if it is a work of the flesh. He blessed Ishmael, the son born after the flesh, and made him a great nation, because of Abraham. The Lord is faithful even when we are unfaithful. But if we want to be a part of the promised seed, or truth, or ministry, we must distinguish between that which is blessed by God and that which is CHOSEN. "Many are called but few are chosen" (MATT.22:14). There are many ministries today which are anointed and blessed, but they are still works of the flesh, having their origin in the mind and strivings of men, and not God. Like Saul, they may lead the church for a time, but they will soon pass into oblivion. While Saul enjoyed the blessing and following of the people, David appeared cursed, and so it is today.

As one of the great tests of David's heart, he proved willing to serve in the house of Saul. He slew the giant for him and fought in his battles, even after he was driven out of the house and Saul was trying to kill him. David did not return evil for evil, but good for evil, just as the coming Messiah who would one day sit on the the throne David established with such character. David obviously viewed the overall well-being of Israel and the purposes of God as more important than his own well-being or recognition. This is in some way a test required of all who would serve the eternal throne of David upon which Christ now sits.

Saul could not long endure the chosen one, just as Ishmael could not endure Issac and taunted him. There is enmity between that which is born of the flesh and that which is born of the spirit. Saul continually tried to kill David, but David would not raise his hand against Saul. He would not take the authority for himself, and he would not try to bring down the works of the flesh who persecuted him. Retaliation and self-promotion will not be found in that which is truly born of God. Those who allow "Saul" to antagonize them into retaliation or self-promotion will find themselves disqualified from leadership in God's chosen ministry.

Possibly the single greatest distinguishing characteristic between Saul and David was found in who they feared the most. When Saul observed the people scattering, and the enemies gathering, he performed the sacrifice even though he had been commanded to wait. He feared the people and the circumstances more than he feared God. When pressed by what must have been one of the greatest trials a man could endure, having his family kidnapped as well as those of all his faithful men, David would not do anything until he had inquired of the Lord, even with his own men threatening to stone him. David feared the Lord more than men or circumstances. Such is the nature of true spiritual authority. Such is the nature of those who have been chosen for leadership during the greatest move of God the earth has ever witnessed.

Not only was David the youngest son in the insignificant house of Jesse, but he was a shepherd, the most humble profession of his day. In the natural, there was nothing in the life of David that would indicate his high calling. It had to be this way. For the kingdom to be built on righteousness it could not be one that attracted those who were drawn by appearances, or who saw prosperity in that which is carnal and temporary. The only ones who would recognize David were those who saw both greatness and prosperity in that which is of the heart, those who loved the truth more than anything this world could give them. It was for this same reason that Jesus was born in a stable.

In Biblical times the stable was a most offensive place. The floors were composed of impacted dung and other filth which had accumulated for decades. The stench was so great they were placed as far away from other dwellings as possible. By today's standards they would not even be fit for animals. That the Lord of Glory would choose such a place to make His entry into this world is one of the more profound revelations of what His message is to man. We would do well not to miss His point as He has not ceased to use such places to make His appearances.

Human reasoning would never lead one to a stable to find God. The only way He could be found was by revelation; only those who were led by the Spirit would come. This has not changed. That which has been born of God is usually repulsive to the pride and presumptions of carnal men.

After His birth Jesus was then raised in the most despised town in the nation. Even His physical appearance was such that no one would be attracted to Him (IS.53:2). He left this world after the most degrading torture and execution yet devised by the base and demented schemes of fallen men. This gospel is foolishness to the natural man, and always will be. It will never attract those who live by human wisdom. Only those who love truth more than anything else in this world will walk with Him in the reproach of the true gospel.

The birth, life and death of Jesus puts the ax to the root of the tree of human wisdom and pride, the fruit of the Tree of Knowledge of Good and Evil. It is the most powerful message the creation has ever heard; it is the most profound testimony of the character and nature of God. When we embellish this gospel to make it appeal to carnal men we destroy its power to set them free, and we ourselves begin to drift from the path of life. For this reason Paul preached nothing but Christ and Him crucified. He knew that if one were to come by any other message it would be a false conversion.

This is a reason for much of the powerlessness of the church today; we converted men to the church, to our doctrines, to our projects and organizations--almost anything but to Christ Himself. We do this because the true gospel is too offensive. We feel that the raw truth of the gospel is doomed to be rejected as foolishness, which is precisely the very power of its message. It is MEANT to be rejected by those who do not love the truth more than their pride. The gospel is meant to be rejected by those who would tend to use it for self-promotion and the approval of men.

This striving for approval is usually quite obvious in ministries driven to expand and grow to "reach the world with the gospel." How many of these have taken the time to reach their own neighbors? One may gain fame throughout the world, do many miracles and cast out many devils, only to come before the Lord and hear that He never knew them. If we would preach only the raw gospel we would be protecting the church from the terrible deceptions and humiliations she has been enduring for almost two millenniums. We would also be protecting the deceivers from a life of delusion in which they believe they are really serving God, that they would not have to hear those terrible words from the Lord on that day, "Depart from Me. I never knew you." How many of the deceivers might have entered into a true salvation had we been faithful not to compromise the gospel message?

If we are to be true ministers we MUST heed the apostle's word: "Have this attitude in yourself which was also in Christ Jesus, who, although He existed in the form of God did not regard equality with God a thing to be GRASPED, but EMPTIED Himself, taking the form of a bond-servant... He HUMBLED Himself, becoming obedient to the point of death, even death on the cross" (PHIL.2:4-8).

Upon entering ministry Jesus emptied Himself and became of no reputation. When we enter ministry with the intention of being filled and making a reputation, we have made a fundamental departure from true ministry. To repeat a most important exhortation for us all: "He who speaks from himself seeks his own glory (or recognition); but he who is seeking the glory of the one who sent him, he is true" (John 7:18).

The recent revelations and shakings in some of the large visible ministries have more purpose than just getting our eyes off of men and back onto the Lord, (though that is important). We have been preaching a false gospel. It does not matter how tearfully someone talks about the cross, if we are not living it is not in our message. Self promotion was the original temptation and it is still one of the most effective in rendering the church and its gospel powerless in bringing about true conversion and true rebirth. The false gospel will swell our church roles and inflate our donations but is repulsive to God. "YOU ARE THOSE WHO JUSTIFY YOUR-

SELVES IN THE SIGHT OF MEN, BUT GOD KNOWS YOUR HEARTS; FOR THAT WHICH IS HIGHLY ESTEEMED AMONG MEN IS DETESTABLE IN THE SIGHT OF GOD" (LUKE 16:15).

That the world is now laughing and scorning the visible church is a just retribution; we must reap what we sow. We wanted the world's recognition and now it has judged us rightly. But there is an invisible church which does not seek the world's recognition or approval. As prophesied, this church has been protected and nourished by God in the wilderness of obscurity (REV. 12:1-6). It has no name or earthly organization. Most of its members do not even understand it; they have wandered about in spiritual caves and holes in the ground. They are sojourners who could not be satisfied with the cities which men build; they keep looking for the one that God has built. Some are true shepherds, some are true wisemen, by revelation they are being led to the stables where the True One is being brought forth once again.

In some of the most humble works and ministries conceivable the God of glory has chosen to bring forth the most powerful men and women of the faith to walk on this earth. To some of the most meek and humble servants a sword has been given that will soon bring to an end the futile works of unbroken religious impostors. Then they will shake the entire world with the true gospel of the kingdom. The whole world is about to understand that He DOES resist the proud, but gives grace to the humble. Those of you who have this hope do not despair, our God is about to arise. But to see Him now, we must go to places that require the death of our flesh and sometimes our reputations. And we must have the heart of Simeon and Anna, who could see in a mere infant the salvation of the world. Don't be discouraged if you don't yet see the fruit; look for the seed that will become the fruit. This does not mean that He is only found in the poor, the wretched and the despised, but that is where He is usually found. "But God has chosen the foolish things of the world to shame the wise, and God has chosen the weak things of the world to shame the things which are strong" (I COR.1:27)

Again there stands One among us who very few really know. He is growing in individuals and works that we would never suspect without a revelation. Those who find Him will no longer care about being known or accepted by men, they will only want to be known by Him. In Him are found all of the treasures of wisdom and knowledge. The knowledge of Him is more valuable than all of the earth's riches. When we know Him all of the wealth and pomp of men seems pitiful. Once we have seen Him we begin to understand why in heaven there is no preaching--just worship! Only after we have been caught up by this worship to walk in heavenly places can we preach the true gospel on earth.

The true gospel will never appeal to the carnal nature of man, it will confront that nature and put the ax to its root. As Paul declared, "IF I WERE STILL TRYING TO PLEASE MEN I WOULD NOT BE A BOND-SERVANT OF CHRIST (GAL.1: 10). We must make a choice as to whom we are going to serve. It will be Christ or mammon, but it will never be both.

We Will Know Them By Their Fruit

Jesus came as a humble carpenter from the most humble town in the most despised nation on earth. Most of those who were called to preach His gospel were "untrained and un-taught." This has never changed, and it will not be changed until the end. The Lord is about to judge the church's tendency to know men according to their credentials, which seminary or Bible school they went to, or even by who laid hands on them, instead of by their fruit. This deception has led to a great portion of the error and darkness which still dominates the church. The Lord warned us against such foolishness, and His ways from the beginning have been a witness against it.

Those who continue in this error will be deceived and become deceivers. Those who do not repent of this will reject those the Lord sends, and approve those He has not sent. From now on we must recognize no man according to the flesh (externals) but according to the spirit. In the days to come the only way we will be able to recognize those who are true messengers will be according to Acts 4:13:

Now as they (the Sanhedrin) observed the confidence of Peter and John, and understood that they were uneducated and untrained men, they were marveling, and began to recognize them AS HAVING BEEN WITH JESUS.

There are no other credentials which are acceptable to the Lord, or that should be acceptable to us. Men's degrees, the schools at which they matriculated, their experience, even their ability to expound the scriptures accurately and articulately, are no basis upon which we should accept or approve anyone. The issue is, have they been with Jesus? Are they ministering Jesus or that which may be true but is in fact the fruit of the Tree of Knowledge?

The Lord's determination to send those who are unacceptable according to the world's standards is a judgement against the world's pride and rebellion; this is the same pride and rebellion which is bringing judgement upon the entire earth. If we do not repent of this we will partake of the world's judgement in this. Even the great apostle Paul, who was learned and trained was displayed in "weakness, and in fear and much trembling." As he told the Galatians, his flesh was a trial to them, yet they received him as an angel (messenger) of God (GAL.4:14). If we are going to receive the truth, and the true ones, we have got to see beyond externals, love the truth more than our pride, and love and openly accept the humble, because God "resists the proud but gives grace to the humble" (JAMES 4:6).

"God has chosen the foolish things of the world to shame the wise, and God has chosen the weak things of the world to shame the things which are strong, and the base things of the world and the despised, God has chosen, the things that are not, that He might nullify the things that are, that no man should boast before God" (I COR.1:27-29).

The day is now come when the Lord will have no more mercy on pride and human presumption. This judgement, like all judgments, will begin with His own household. He is once again crying over His own people: "O Jerusalem, Jerusalem, who kills the prophets and stones those who are sent to her! How often I wanted to gather your children together, the way a hen gathers her chicks under her wings, and you were unwilling. Behold, your house is being left to you desolate! For I say to you, FROM NOW ON YOU SHALL NOT SEE ME UNTIL YOU SAY, "BLESSED IS HE WHO COMES IN THE NAME OF THE LORD!" (MATT.23:37-39)

We will not see Him again until we see Him in those whom He sends. The church is just as guilty now as Jerusalem was then. Time after time He tried to gather us together and we stoned those He sent to help us. But rest assured, there is soon to be a people who will not judge by what their eyes see. These will know no man according to externals and doctrines, but after the Spirit. These will recognize Him and receive Him, in everyone in whom He dwells. These will be gathered under His wings and protected from the onslaught to come.

The only Biblical protection against deluding influences is to have a love for the Truth. Only those who keep their first love will escape deception in these times. If we have any other motive for following Him we will be in jeopardy. Selfish ambition, fear of hell, the need to be identified with a strong social entity, idealism, the need to please others, love for the excitement and miracles, seeking God's provision, or any other reason, will prove to be inadequate foundations for our faith.

Almost every deception is rooted in the original lie the serpent used to deceive Eve--that we can become like God without God. Delusions will turn the focus of our attention upon ourselves, just as they did when our first parents ate of that deadly fruit and then looked at themselves. These things have not changed from the beginning.

Most delusions will be based on an element of truth. Satan still comes as an "angel of light," or "messenger of truth." Just because something is true does not mean that it is life. The "good" side of the Tree of Knowledge looks good because it IS good, but human goodness is motivated by self-righteousness and self-promotion. For this reason the "Pharisee of Pharisees" who was "according to the Law, found blameless," persecuted the Way unto death. The "sinners" almost never persecute the church, and as the Lord Himself testified, the publicans and harlots will enter the kingdom before the upstanding citizens who are self-righteous.

Because delusions can be based in truth we will seldom be able to identify them merely by their compliance with Scripture. Satan quotes scripture to deceive, just as he did to Jesus. We can judge only by the fruit. Where does the teaching focus our attention? Does it glorify the Lord or men. Regardless of how often and how emotionally we may use His name, selfish ambition is still selfish ambition, and it will inevitably lead to deception.

In the days to come there will be men performing miracles and demonstrating great power, in order to testify of and verify their ministries, just as there have been for many years. There is another kind of minister coming who will perform even greater works, but will not even care to have people know who they are. Publicity will be a burden to them, not a thrill. They will not seek attention for themselves, or their ministries, but for the One who sent them. These are true messengers. These will have no desire for building great organizations, but rather with building great people, which has been the heart of God from the beginning. Like Abraham, those who see the city which God is building out of living stones will not be distracted by the projects contrived by ambitious men.

When the fire of tribulation comes it will not be our discipline, our submission, or even our knowledge of the truth that keeps us faithful; the only thing that will keep us is our LOVE for Truth, Himself. This cannot be over-emphasized. In the end, everyone will quit except for those in love. When our love grows cold that is when we drift. If we are giving ourselves to seek anything in this day it should be the Father's love for the Son, and the Son's love for the Father. This must be the WHOLE focus of our attention. If we do not see, and hold in our vision, the central purpose of God to sum up all things IN His Son, then we are forever in danger of being consumed by the lesser purposes of God, or even worse distractions.

As the apostle Paul explained, in what may be the greatest summation of true apostolic vision: "ONE THING I do; forgetting what lies behind and reaching forward to what lies ahead,

I press on toward the goal for the prize of the HIGH CALL-ING of God in Christ Jesus" (PHIL. 3:13-14). Jesus IS the high calling of God. Being found in Him is our purpose. This statement may be the fundamental issue which separates true apostles from pretenders; the true apostle keeps his vision focused on ONE THING, the Father's love for His Son and presenting all men complete IN HIM.

When we are concentrated upon the primary purpose of God, the secondary purposes will all then serve the One. If our eye is single, on Him, then the whole body will be full of light. If our eye is not single, but divided into the many secondary purposes, they will become darkness instead of light. Even though they may be truths, they will still deceive us. Deception is not just misunderstanding truth, it is not being in His will; it is not doing what He called us to do. This is why Satan often comes as an angel of light, or messenger of truth. Satan is able to deceive those who have truth, but he cannot deceive those who have a "love for the truth" (see II THES.2:5-10). Only when we have a love for the truth do we believe in our hearts and not just with our heads. It is those who believe in their hearts who shall be saved.

A coming emphasis in the church will be humility. The Lord knows how desperately we need this emphasis. But humility, like submission, is not always what it appears. Saul was "small in his own eyes," a humble man by almost any Biblical interpretation. But is a man really humble if he can make a decision which will effect thousands of the Lord's own children without even consulting Him? What appeared to be humility was really insecurity. Insecurity can quickly become presumption, which it often does in over-reaction to cir-cumstances and fears.

Insecurity mixed with authority has led to some of the most presumptuous acts in history; because of it a number of despots have slaughtered millions for the sake of self preserva-tion. It was because of insecurity that Saul slew the Lord's own priests and tried desperatly to kill David. It is a false doctrine which teaches that humility is the fruit of losing security in ourselves or the world. True humility comes from gaining the understanding and trust in who God is. The first is still of the Tree of Knowledge; the latter is the Tree of Life.

The former still has our attention on ourselves; the latter upon the living God.

Pride does lead to a fall, and the Lord resists the proud, but if we start judging who is proud and who is humble according to a doctrine, we will almost certainly find ourselves judging the Lord's chosen and receiving that which is born of the flesh. Even the great prophet Samuel was prone to this error. One would think that after the debacle with Saul he would not again judge after the flesh. But upon going to the house of Jesse to anoint God's chosen vessel, he immediately thought that the son who was the most physically imposing was the one. He was mistaken, and so are we time after time because of the same inclination.

Do not be awed or inspired by the knowledgeable, the articulate, the dynamic performers and speakers who draw great crowds; rather fear for their souls. Even if we draw multitudes and have great success in our ministry by fulfilling the purposes of God, every man of God will be the most vulnerable when enjoying success and human approval. That is when he needs our prayers the most. "Take heed when you think you stand, lest you fall" (I COR.10:12).

It is easier to require truth from someone than to require life from them. It is easy to know all about the Lord and still not know Him. We may know all about Him but still be "worshipping an unknown God." Having right doctrines will not deliver us from the fire that is coming--we must know Him as our Life.

MATT.7:13-24
HEB.3:4-14

CHAPTER 5

THE PERSECUTION

Before the ingathering Christianity will experience a great humiliation. The enemy's strategy is to so utterly degrade the church that she will begin to retreat just as she is about to make one of her greatest advances. The "accuser of the brethren" will go forth with unprecedented rage against the Body of Christ. The "revelations" of immoral and unethical behavior by hundreds of highly visible ministries will bring about a loathing of Christianity throughout the world, for a time. These revelations will include such things as child molesting, rape, and the most vile forms of perversion. Some of these will be true, but MOST WILL NOT BE TRUE.

There has never been a more critical time for the church to walk in and trust the gift of discernment of spirits. In many cases, even when all of the evidence appears irrefutable, it will be an entrapment and the accused will be innocent. Some of those who will appear as champions of righteousness by exposing others to "cleanse the temple" will be deceivers who helped set up the entrapments. We must know each other after the Spirit, not rumors, or even what appears to be hard evidence.

Satan's hit list includes hundreds of Christian leaders. It will begin against some who have recently made mistakes which were publicly exposed, but the new charges will be contrived about even worse failings and perversions. After an atmosphere of revulsion is created, the enemy will then move against even the most respected Evangelical, Pentecostal and Charismatic leaders with charges of the most base forms of perversion and ethical failures.

In conjunction with this hoards of cults and satanic worshippers will begin attacking congregations and meetings. They will enter services in mass, spitting on people, urinating and performing lude acts in order to humiliate the church. This practice will be publicized until it becomes a fad among the cults. What begins as a few isolated incidents will soon become common throughout the world. Again, the enemy's strategy is to so utterly humiliate the church that it will retreat and go into hiding, thus thwarting the coming move of God.

It is an age old tactic of the enemy to try to devour what God is bringing forth while it is still in its infancy. We see this in REV.12:1-6 as the dragon waited for the woman to give birth so that he might devour the child. We see this principle with the birth of Moses and the enemy's attempt to destroy the deliverer by destroying the male infants of Israel. This was a prophetic parallel of the enemy's strategy to destroy the infant Jesus in the same way. We also see this in the enemy's attempt to destroy a coming last day ministry through abortion.

The Lord is allowing this onslaught for His own purposes. He is going to have a pure and holy church. In the first century it was a noble thing to desire a position of leadership in the church. Those who did were putting their lives and families in jeopardy. This is still true throughout much of the world. But in the West a church leader now has more in common with a corporate executive than its Biblical counterpart. Instead of having the same mind that was in Christ Jesus, who "emptied Himself... and became of no reputation," church leadership has often been used as one of the most vile forms of self-promotion. This is about to end forever.

There are sincere and devoted men of God in positions of leadership, but there are many who have attained such positions through political manipulation and self-promotion. To these church leadership is merely another profession rather than a calling. These will not be able to stand the humiliation which is coming, fleeing to demonstrate that they were in fact hirelings, not serving in devotion to the Lord but for their own personal interests.

Some of those who were called and appointed by God will also be humiliated and found powerless at times to deal with the onslaught. But these will not run. Their failures will result in a greater determination to know the truth of God's delegated authority over the evil one. By this they will be delivered from hindering delusions and begin to walk in a power and authority never before experienced. The enemy's strategy of humiliating the saints into retreat will actually work to purify the ranks and inculcate in the faithful a greater resolve.

This humiliation will ultimately reduce the church to a figurative Gideon's 300. Like Gideon's little band, who could stand no longer the humiliation of Israel at the hands of Midian, these will be pushed to the limit of what they can tolerate. They will then take their little lights and trumpets and attack the entire camp of the enemy, beginning the rout. Then, many of those who have departed out of fear and confusion will return, helping to complete the victory to bring in a great harvest. Everything that is lost to the enemy during his onslaught will be regained and much more.

The church's posture towards this coming slander must be a determination for us to indeed humble ourselves under the mighty hand of God, but not man or Satan. The Lord "resists the proud, but gives grace to the humble." We must not let the revelations of sin drive us into hiding, but rather to the throne of grace. We need not hide from or deny the true failures, but confess them and repent of our evil. The Lord's ultimate victory over the accuser will be so great that the church will be esteemed and marveled at by the entire world very soon after the peak of her humiliation. But the church's exaltation will not come because we have started to look better in the sight of man, but because we will have embraced the cross and allowed the humiliation to drive us to the throne of grace, and God will then lift us up. What the world thinks of the church will have nothing to do with her exaltation or humiliation, but what God alone thinks determines her fate.

When the church comes out of this period she will have a changed concept of both humility and exaltation. We will never again use the world's opinion of us as a barometer of our condition. The church's exaltation will not come from public opinion, but from above. The New Jerusalem comes down from heaven; she is not lifted up from below. When we cease to care what the world thinks of us, and are wholly occupied with what God thinks of us, He will then pour out a grace upon us that is irresistable even to our most vehement enemies, which cannot be prevailed upon by any power of darkness.

It is important that we use this opportunity to embrace the discipline of the Lord. Nevertheless, He has given this revelation "in order that no advantage be taken of us by Satan; for WE ARE NOT IGNORANT OF HIS SCHEMES" (II COR.2:11). As sensational as this may presently seem, the Lord has revealed an unholy alliance which involves major denominations, criminal factions, even some government officials and agencies. The following is the scenario which will actually take place:

Hundreds of millions of dollars stand to be made from the slanderous articles and transfer of property resulting from the failure of major ministries. Any time potential for this kind of money transfer arises evil men get involved. Because of the money lost by having their publications removed from some of their more effective outlets, major pornography publishers will have a vendetta against specific ministries and Christians in general. These have been accumulating real information against some ministries; they have contrived false testimonies from paid witnesses against others. Their plan for releasing the stories is systematic and strategic for making the most on the publicity and the property transfers.

Some denominations will get involved seeing this as a chance to eliminate what they consider "the fringe element" of Christianity. These feel that the popular evangelicals, charismatics and televangelists have deprived them of resources and support. Some of these denominational officials have no fear of God and are well aware of what they are doing. Others honestly feel they are doing God a favor.

Some government officials and agencies see this humiliation of Christianity as a way to eliminate the tax exempt status of ministries and possibly even the entire church, with popular support. This alone could erase the deficit without raising taxes. Major churches and ministries will be the target of audits and investigations. Many of these officials are sincere in wanting to eradicate impostors who bilk the public, and the government, of substantial resources. Others, some of whom will show increasingly pious facades, are out to destroy the conservative Christian political clout. Others are outright anti-Christ.

A number of prophets and ministers to whom the Lord has revealed this information, and who have faithfully begun to warn the church, have already had their lives and/or ministries threatened. Let us not be disturbed by these things. We are now coming to some of the most serious and difficult times in human history. As the prophet Daniel foretold:

And forces from him will arise, desecrate the sanctuary fortress, and do away with the regular sacrifice. And they will set up the abomination of desolation.

And by smooth words he will turn to godlessness those who act wickedly toward the covenant, BUT THE PEOPLE WHO KNOW THEIR GOD WILL DISPLAY STRENGTH AND TAKE ACTION.

And those who have insight among the people will give understanding to the many; yet they will fall by the sword and by flame, by captivity and by plunder, for many days (DAN.11:31-33).

We live in enemy territory; "the whole world lies in the power of the evil one" (I JOHN 5:19). We must not continue to judge each other by information received from the enemy's own media. The love of many will grow cold. It is time for the faithful to walk by the Spirit and to know each other only after the Spirit. Let us not be beguiled from the simplicity of devotion to Christ. We must seek first His kingdom and His purposes. Those following the Lord out of selfish ambition, who make decisions because of personal or political considerations will soon betray the faith, and the faithful.

Those who are given understanding of the enemy's schemes will be made primary targets for entrapments in order to discredit their warnings. Some will "fall by the sword (murder) and captivity (imprisonment)." But those who know their God will not retreat; they will "display strength and take action," regardless of the consequences. This is a war and there will be casualties. Those who fall by the sword and the entrapments, are martyrs to the Lord and He will keep that which they have entrusted to Him. We must not be concerned about what men, even the church, may think of us. "The Lord knows those who are His." Those who are conformed to the image of the Lord's death, alone and deserted by even His own followers, will soon come again in the power of His resurrection. Those who give their lives will be seed for the greatest victory over evil and ingathering of souls ever accomplished through the church.

This will be a period of some of the darkest and most confusing days for the faithful. Some who have appeared to be the strongest and most faithful, will fall. Some of these will betray great numbers of saints to authorities while trying to save their own lives and reputations. This has been going on since the beginning throughout much of the world, but will be a great shock to believers who are accustomed to religious freedom.

During this time paranoia would sweep the church were it not for the courage and boldness of individuals who refuse to retreat in the face of this onslaught. Some who are now considered mere "privates in God's army" are about to become some of the greatest heroes of the faith in the last day church. These will take a stand while others are retreating, refusing to be moved by the onslaught of the enemy. Their courage will give courage to a few more, who will each strengthen a few more, until the lines hold and the raging enemy will be stopped. Then the entire body of Christ will go on the offensive, completely routing its enemies. Then all of the fear and paranoia the enemies of Christ used against the church will flood their own souls.

Truth Is Stronger Than Lies

Just when it appears that the harvest is over and the spirit of antichrist has prevailed, the church will rise to her greatest victory. What is left of the previous revivals will have been pruned back to only a stump, but this little stump will bring forth shoots of life that will then fill the earth. The truth will begin to burn again. Like a spark lit in a dry wood, it will burn and burn until all of the wood, hay and stubble in the entire world is aflame. The little stone (of Daniel's prophecy) will strike the feet of iron and clay--the alliance of church and state. The remnants of all of the world's empires and humanistic philosophies will begin to crumble, while the little rock begins to prevail in every nation on earth. Truth uttered by the faithful will be impacting the world like great shock waves, leveling the mountains (governments) and hills (cults and societies), raising up and empowering the oppressed.

The Lord will use the persecutions to shake the church from the dust and to prepare her for the work ahead. Persecution will separate the faithful from the false. It will help turn our theories and principles into the reality of true spiritual life. It will turn some of the most pompous and erudite Biblical expounders and theorists into spiritual beggars. Some of the most humble and ignorant believers will be transformed into giants of the faith whose steadfastness will lead multitudes into kingdom of God.

Some of the qualities which bring men into prominence in the peaceful, wealthy and unpersecuted church, will disqualify them when the fire comes. When the fire of tribulation comes we will see many of our present leaders deserting and a different class of believer will take their place. It will then require sacrifice to lead, and only true servants will lay down their lives to make that sacrifice.

This is not to imply that all members of the present leadership has presumed to that position. Some are true servants and have been both called and appointed. These have not used politics and manipulation to attain their positions, but have faithfully waited for God to open every door, which they walked through with fear and trembling before Him. Those who have walked uprightly during the times of compromise and self-seeking will prove to be some of the strongest leaders of all when the fire of persecution comes.

Even some of the most sincere and pure in the ministry are destined to succumb to moral and ethical failures. Many of these will be destroyed by their sins. Some, like David who fell to one of the most grievous transgressions recorded, will be restored to even greater spiritual authority.

It is important that we not dilute the Biblical standards for discipline in dealing with sin in the church, or the requirements for those who we are to accept as leaders. But it is just as crucial that we know each other after the Spirit and not the flesh, the heart and not just externals. The Lord knew that sin was in David's heart when He called him, that under the right circumstances he would fall. He loved and used David before the fall, and after it. Not only did David fall to adultery, he murdered one of his most devoted and loyal men to cover it up. Even this was not greater than the grace of God, and after this David had a revelation of grace which may have exceeded any other Old Covenant prophet. In the days to come we will all have to be vessels of grace and restoration, because we will all need it.

While attending a prophetic conference recently I was with a brother I have known for years would be a significant prophet to the last day church. This brother has been rejected by much of the church because of the status of his marriage, which has been one of many difficulties, and at this time was in separation. One night the Lord spoke to me about my own marriage, which I consider to be in compliance with Biblical standards. He said that this other man was more righteous in complying with His mandate for marriage standards than I was. He proceeded to show me how I had been given a godly wife who loved and sought Him, and that the condition of my marriage was purely the result of grace. I had given little effort to comply with His madate in this, and have been hard, unyeilding and resistant to things He would have me do to improve my marriage. Against the most humiliating circumstances and resistance, this other man had for years devoted himself to complying with the Biblical mandate and making his marriage work, even when he had every right, both Biblical and moral, to have walked away from it. Yet, the church has judged him as a failure and me as acceptable in this area. God has a very different opinion.

As stated, this is not to detract from the Biblical standards which are given for a reason, but the letter kills when it is not used by the Spirit. How many of us would not have disfellowshipped David after the incident with Bathsheba, only to have later followed Absolom into deception and defeat along with the rest of Israel. Israel was led astray by Absalom because they walked after the flesh, judging by externals, instead of by the Spirit. We must seek the heart of Zadok the priest, who did not regard David by his successes or failures, but by the anointing and commission of God, and remained faithful even when all of Israel went astray.

God's grace usually exceeds what men are able to comprehend or extend. But let us also understand that even though David was forgiven and restored, he still had to reap what was sown. He and his family paid a terrible price for his few moments of passing pleasure, and so will we. We can be restored if we fall, but it will be much easier for us, our families, and congregations, if we resist and stand.

Even some who have denied and betrayed their brothers will repent and be restored. Some who have experienced the greatest failures will love the Lord more because they will have been forgiven of more. These will give their lives for some of the great victories of the faith. Persecution will bring paranoia upon pretenders in the faith, but those who are real will grow in strength and trust. These will not become closed to people because of the persecution, but more open, taking greater and greater chances with their lives in order to lead others to Christ, or to heal and restore the fallen. Fire purifies the gold; it only burns the wood, hay and straw. During the times of greatest hate we will see demonstrations of the greatest love; during times of the greatest fear we will see the greatest champions of faith stand up.

Because many will stumble during these times of incredible pressure, we must distinguish the difference between remorse and repentance. The confusion over this issue has kept the church in much bondage and weakness. Judas felt remorse; Peter repented. It's not repentance to feel bad because we were caught, or even to sincerely feel bad about the sin. Repentance is to turn away from the sin and to accept the propitiation of the cross for it. The Lord could have forgiven Judas for his betrayal; that was not the unforgivable sin. We are probably all guilty of betraying Him; as we have done unto the least of His we have done it unto Him. What made Judas incorrigible was that he hung himself; he tried to pay the price for his own sin. Whenever we "hang ourselves" by trying to carry our own guilt, we are saying in effect that the cross just was not adequate to pay for our sin, that we must pay for this one ourselves. This does not strengthen our resistance to sin, it weakens it. The messages of repentance and restoration soon to permeate the church are in preparation for the dark times ahead. We must not go on hanging ourselves, or others.

Even the greatest spiritual leaders are but flesh. Peter opened the church age with one of its most powerful messages, opened the door of faith to the gentiles, and had been one of the most intimate of the Lord's disciples, had to be rebuked by Paul because "he stood condemned" (GAL.2:11). He was not being straightforward about the same gospel. Men are most vulnerable to a fall after great spiritual victories. Immediately after Peter had his great revelation about Jesus being the Messiah, Jesus called him "Satan" for setting his mind on man's interests (MATT. 16:13-23). Just like everyone else, leaders stumble in many ways. Our faith cannot be built upon any man, doctrine, or church, but upon the Lord Himself. He alone will never disappoint us. Those who provide leadership in these times will be under the greatest pressure, and will need a generous measure of grace and support.

In what are presently some of the most free countries, the time is coming when the penalty for owning or possessing a Bible or religious book will be prison or death. Though this may seem devastating, it will not in any way thwart or even slow down the furtherance of the gospel. All things do work to the good of those who love the Lord, even this.

The Bible is a most wonderful and precious gift; it is His personal letter to us, written by the blood and tears of the best men this world has ever known, but He never meant for it to take His place in our lives. The early church did not have the Bible; if a congregation had even one scroll of an Old Testament book they were blessed, yet we have not even attained to the power of their faith. They were dependent on a living relationship with the Lord for their guidance, which is the way it is meant to be. He did not say that when He went away He would leave us a book to lead us into all truth, but the Holy Spirit. It is not just knowing the book of the Lord that should be our goal, but knowing the Lord of the book. If we know Him losing our Bibles will not affect our faith because we have the author of the Bible living within us.

Today we have Bibles, books, tapes and a host of other

aids, which we must take full advantage of while we have them. Soon we will grieve over the time we wasted on worthless T.V. programs, frivolous magazines or other diversions when we could have given ourselves to the Word. But we must guard against having our faith dependent on the letter in place of the Spirit. It was the Spirit Who was given to guide, comfort and teach us. He will continue to do His job regardless of what aids we have or do not have.

Communist Advances

There will be many changes in communism, and the world will have a brief respite from the unrelenting assault of the red tide, but then it will make further significant advances. South Korea, the Philipeans, South and Central America, including Mexico, and most of Africa will be swept up by it. The U.S. will have a "hot" border to the south with almost daily clashes and casualties. Internal pressures will have caused such a lack of resolve that she will even give up large sections of her own territory to invaders by failing to use the force required to stop them. At that time the enemies within will be greater than those without.

In some of the countries taken by the communists there will be an attempt to completely wipe out Christianity, as well as other religions. At the same time, in some communist countries religious tolerance will increase, but seldom to the degree that it could be considered true religious freedom. In the nations that remain "free" or democratic, religious intolerance will increase until believers will be in some degree of danger in every nation on earth.

The most severe persecution against believers will come in countries which now enjoy religious freedom. A number of these governments will have aligned themselves with the false church. This false church will have allegiance and authority over most of the populations of what is left of the "free world." This church will incite governments and populations against all Christians who do not submit to its authority.

The unfolding in some communist countries will have been very different than the scenario above. The false church will not have gained political power in most of these. Often in reaction to the false church, these governments will have given great liberty to true believers, who will labor in the harvest in relative peace, their dark night already turned into day. Powerful apostolic teams will come out of Russia and China giving strength to the persecuted church throughout the world.

The great changes that are sweeping the world will bring many changes to communist doctrine, theory and practice, as well as that of capitalism, free enterprise and democracy. We must not be overly encouraged or discouraged by these changes. "The whole world lies in the power of the evil one." It is not communism, nor capitalism that is the enemy, but humanism. This includes every "ism" as they all have their root in the Tree of The Knowledge of Good and Evil. The great changes and clashes which are coming in human philosophies will bring a more clear distinction between the light and darkness. It will be during the confusion of these times that the church makes her greatest advances in attaining the life and power in which she was called to walk. The church will be abiding so close to her Lord during these times that she will give almost no attention to what is going on in the world, except as they might relate to opportunities for spreading the gospel.

Preparation For Persecution

There will be world-wide "house church" and "Christian community" movements which will help prepare the saints for both the persecution and the harvest. These actually were begun in the 1960's, but often floundered and failed. The reason for many of the failures was the same as for the discipleship and other movements--they were built upon a doctrine instead of a commission. Like the crowning of Israel's first king, men of vision started to see the need, but often raced ahead of the Lord's timing for their implementation.

Few Christians can read the book of Acts without longing for the same kind of church life. Some allowed their idealism to move them to try and duplicate it. But this kind of church life can only be duplicated if it is initiated the same way that it was in Jerusalem. The Jerusalem church experienced a wonderful community because community was not their emphasis. Their attention was on the Lord who moved among them. As the Lord begins to move as dynamically in our midst we too will be unified into a true community of spirit, but possibly without even knowing it. The Jerusalem church met from house to house because when the Lord is moving all His people want to do is meet. These things happened spontaneously. There is a big difference in doing something because it is a doctrine and doing it because the Lord is moving so powerfully we are swept up in it. When the Lord is in His temple the temple will not be what gets our attention! We will care very little about what we are doing; we will have all of our attention on the wonderful things He is doing and just move with the Pillar of Fire.

Communities and house churches started because of idealism or doctrines have almost all failed. Many of those which still exist are dead, continuing to exist on artificial life support instead of true spiritual life. Even though they continue to have some of the vital signs, remove the machinery and they too will expire. Many who were hurt by these failures do not want to even hear the words "Christian community," or "house church" again, but were taken through these experiences to be used by the Lord for what is coming. Much of their revelation is in what not to do, but their experience will often save others years of time spent having to learn the same things. Everyone who has been through the fire of failure, who keeps seeking the Lord and pressing on, will have their failures turned into spiritual authority that will move mountains for others. Just weeks after Peter denied the Lord he testified of His Lordship with such authority the greatest powers of his nation would marvel at him. The Lord will do the same for all who just keep going and refuse to let their failures stop them.

As the intensity of this next move of God picks up, Christian communities will be birthed with people hardly realizing it. The focus of these will not be "community life," but doing all things for the sake of the gospel. The community will just be a means of becoming more efficient in the labors of the harvest. Life in the communities will be both more wonderful and more difficult than expected, but more importantly, they will serve God's purposes.

Some communities will serve as refuges for persecuted Christians and Jews. The fear of the Lord will come upon intruders to such a degree no one will enter their gates with impure motives. At some of these, mobs or soldiers approaching them will be struck blind, or have their eyes opened to see angelic guards, causing them to flee in panic. Those established by the Lord will be protected. This does not mean that they will not have problems, even serious ones. We have been told that it is "through many tribulations we must enter the kingdom of God" (ACTS 14:22). In His will tribulations are not obstacles, they are gateways into His kingdom. We're entering days when everyone will have tribulation; those who count it joy will have great joy, and a peace that will cause a world in turmoil to marvel and seek their God.

As saints gather spontaneously in one another's houses and community centers, home churches will be born. A great anointing will be upon these home meetings and some of the greatest visitations of the Lord will take place in them. Leaders and ministries will be raised up through them just as Stephen was in the first church. Some will even send out apostolic teams. Large congregations will be giving themselves to making home meetings the very center of church life. Even without knowing it, most of these are being prepared for the time when all large meetings will be banned, or the targets of violence and persecution.

Every congregation which is not effectively "equipping the saints for the work of service" will find itself being scattered and disbanded. The church will not continue to be a big sheep pen where they are just fed and entertained. In the eyes of the Spirit no congregation is seen by its buildings or other works, but by the maturity of its individual members. Every ministry which has buried its talent for equipping the saints is about to have it taken away and given to those who are using theirs efficiently. The rise and fall of many will be because of this one issue. The Lord is about to curse every "tree" which is not bearing fruit. Fruit bears the seed for reproduction. If a ministry is not reproducing itself it is not bearing fruit. Those who allow the people to depend too much on them, will be judged. The Lord will not continue tolerating self-serving and self-promoting leadership. The church will soon need a thousand times the ministry it now has. This ministry must be prepared for service now.

True discipleship will be restored to effectively prepare a great army of leaders. As the congregations are scattered by persecution, the people will be scattered abroad like seed, multiplying their fruitfulness. When a leader is removed a host will arise to take his place. Every attack against the church will result in an advance for the gospel. Preparation for this resilience is being made now, and will increase in earnest until the body of Christ takes on the seriousness and determination of an army marching to battle.

As great multitudes start coming to the Lord, it is important that these are in fact being converted and are not just being swept in by the excitement. Those who are being converted to the church, personalities, doctrines, or to have their needs met, will often become betrayers during persecution. A church's tendency to make it too easy for inclusion will cost many lives. We must not make it overly difficult, or become suspicious of every new believer, but we must come to trust the gift of discernment of spirits, and we must insist on real conversion before admittance to the holy assembly. There is only one Door to the church. We must insist that no one enter except through Him. A door is used to both let people in AND keep them out when necessary.

Cults And Pop Religions

There will be an increase of cults, satanic worshippers and pop religions proclaiming the beginning of a new age. Some of these will be mere intellectual diversions, some will be fueled by demonic powers performing extraordinary supernatural wonders. Though they will capture the attention of the multitudes and often ridicule and deride the saints, they are not the greatest threat, or even a significant deterrent to the move of God. In fact, some of these will be fertile fields from which a great harvest will be reaped. Many who are in these movements are poor in spirit, seeking spiritual answers to their problems and heart's yearnings, and have accurately perceived and rejected the shallowness of the visible church. These are seeking a reality with the power to live in these difficult times, and the Lord wants to give it to them.

As stated previously, there will be increasing attacks upon churches and congregations from satanic worshippers. They will enter meetings, demanding to be baptized as a mockery and scorning the leaders openly. There will be such an onslaught of this type that it will cause many to flee from the ministry because of their fear of these confrontations. This is the Lord's doing. It will separate those who have presumed a position without His commissioning. Only those who have the calling and walk by His authority will stand this onslaught; the rest will flee naked and wounded like the Jewish exorcists who tried to cast out demons in the name of Jesus whom Paul knew.

Those who are commissioned by the Lord will come to a place where they are not intimidated by any spirit, and will cast them out with great demonstrations of the power of God. Not only will this increase the faith of the saints, but lead many in the world who have suffered at the hands of these cults to flee to Jesus for refuge. After a time of confrontation, those in the cults will flee in great fear at the approach of Christians, and attacks from this source will then become rare.

During the initial stages of the harvest there will be a great reaping among the Jehovah's Witnesses, Mormons, Seventh Day Adventists, and other sects in which there is a doctrinal mixture. These will be won by love, not truth. Some of these will become great teachers, having come to love the truth with an unquenchable zeal because of their previous delusions and bondage. Others will become tireless, faithful laborers for the harvest. The whole body of Christ will be blessed by those who come from these groups. Some will need a lot of ministry and teaching, but this effort on their behalf will pay great dividends for the kingdom, just as it did with the Pharisee of Pharisees who became the uncompromising apostle of grace.

Cults and sects have been very busy planning their coming assaults upon the church, but the Lord has His generals planning a strategy against them. The Lord's strategy is not defensive in nature, but offensive. He is going to release powerful young evangelists who will convert multitudes from these cults. Like Elijah, some of these will at times take a stand against a hoard of false prophets, scattering them all by the power of the One Who works in them.

The Mystery Of Iniquity

There are a number of "mysteries" on which the scriptures give a great deal of understanding. There are two of which the Bible give us little understanding; the mystery of godliness, and the mystery of iniquity. The Lord left these as true mysteries because of the tendency of the immature to carry each of them to extremes. Godliness can become iniquity when reduced to law, and the iniquity of the legalistic is even more destructive than the iniquity of carnality. Religious legalism has been the most deadly force in human history, and it will be till the end.

It is not yet time to speak in depth of the "mystery of iniquity," but there are a couple of details which we do need to understand, both of which are generally misunderstood at this time. Possibly the greatest understanding of this mystery is given by Paul in his letter to the Thessalonians:

> Let no man deceive you by any means: for that day (the day of the Lord) shall not come, except there come a falling away first, and   that man of sin be revealed, the son of perdition;

> Who opposes and exalts himself above all that is called God, or that is worshipped; so that he, as God, sitteth in the temple of God, showing himself that he is God.....
> And now you know what restrains him that he might be revealed in his time.

> For the mystery of iniquity IS ALREADY AT WORK; only he who now restrains will do so until he is taken out of the way. (II THES.2:3-7)

97

The falling away discussed by Paul started to take place shortly after his death and continued for the next few centuries until the church was plunged into what we now historically view as the "Dark Ages." There is still a time in the last day when "the love of many will grow cold," but that is not what the apostle is here referring to.

The "temple" in which the son of perdition is to take his seat is not a building, as the temple is no longer one made with hands, but is in fact the church, the present temple of God.

In The Revelation, John made an appeal to those who have wisdom, that they might calculate the number of the beast, "for the number is that of a MAN, and his number is six hundred and sixty-six" (REV.13:18). Since this revelation was first given to the church Christians have been on the lookout for someone to come along and try to stamp them with a 666. This is the result of our shallow understanding of certain crucial factors which are now coming to fruition in the earth. Whether or not this is a literal mark is NOT the important issue here. Receiving a mark is not a sin. The sin is to worship the beast; the mark is merely evidence that one has in fact been worshipping it. Will we be free of the wrath of God if we refuse to take a mark but partake of the spirit of the beast everyday? Those who are of his spirit will not be able to refuse the mark or anything else from this beast even if they know full well what it is. Likewise, if we are free from the spirit of this beast we would not take a mark, whether literal or metaphorically, or anything else from him, even if we do not know what it is.

True wisdom is to understand the MEANING of that number. Six is the number of MAN (i.e. man was created on the sixth day, etc..). That this is three sixes indicates that this is man trying to stand in the place of the Godhead. This is the ultimate harvest of the first sin when man partook of the forbidden fruit so that he could be like God, without God. We see that this beast "comes up out of the earth" because it is the result of the "seed of Cain" being "tillers of the ground," or earthly minded. If we follow the unfolding stream of every human philosophy, religion and idealogy, we can see a pattern in which they all flow together and meet at this final common position. Just as the streams which make glad the city of God all flow together and make one river of life at the end, so too will all of the streams of man's rebellion flow together in a river of death at the end.

The ultimate rebellion and mockery is for the man of sin, who is the personification of the sin of man, to take his seat in the church, the very temple of God, claiming to be the head of the church taking Christ's rightful place, seemingly fulfilling man's ultimate ambition to take God's place. Every church, ministry, denomination or movement which is in fact headed by men or human organization in place of Christ will easily succumb to this ultimate blasphemy. These will never suspect that this is anything but God exalting their own human effort and ingenuity. As the apostle told the intellectuals of Athens, "human hands cannot serve Him." His work is not by might, power or intellectual prowess, but only the Spirit can beget that which is Spirit.

The issue of Jesus being the Head is the most important issue of this age. Just as the Lord's mark which He places upon His bondservants is not a literal visible mark, that which the beast is placing upon men is far more subtle than we have been led to believe. The mark of the beast is upon men's minds and their works (forehead and hands). If he does come one day with a literal mark it will only be an indication of that which he has done in men's hearts, and those men will not refuse it even if they know what it is.

In this day the greatest threat and deception of the enemy is not coming from that which is overtly evil, but that which actually appears good and righteous. Satan's most deadly form is as the "angel of light." The fruit that brought death was from the Tree the of Knowledge of Good and Evil. It is the good side of that tree that Satan is coming to try and deceive us with. Its fruit looks good and has all of the appearance of wisdom, but it kills just as surely as the evil side. It kills because it is human goodness offered as a compensation for our evil conscience, replacing the cross and therefore Jesus as our Head and the Source of our life.

To the true works of God, the onslaught by the cults does not present a threat. There will be some humiliations and embarassments caused by it, but this will only work to strengthen and give greater determination to the saints. The demons quickly acknowledged and bowed the knee to Jesus and His apostles. Occasionally they would be an annoyance, but not a threat. It was the religious and upstanding citizens who persecuted and crucified the Lord, and His followers. It will be the same in the days to come. The greatest persecution against the advancing church will come from the moral and conservative people and their religious institutions. This is where the "son of perdition" will actually take his seat declaring himself to be god, an action which is to be far more subtle than most are expecting. The day will come when those who call themselves Christians will consider it their duty to God and society to kill the true believers. We need not fear demons; they fear us. Be wary of the religious establishment.

The false church will have sweeping political power but its popular support will be superficial. For a time most of its attacks against true Christians will be directed against the leadership, just as was the case in the first century. Then, for a time, there will be such an inflow of converts that the advancing church will not be able to contain them all. Many of the former works and traditional churches will be swelled with the overflow. Because of this they will assert that they are both the cause and primary purpose for the revival. This delusion will not last long because the tribulation in the world will eventually consume every religious institution built by man, including the false church. This is the judgement of the Lord against the works He did not commission: The great "sea," or mass humanity, which they sought to rule, will rise up to destroy them. As they are collapsing they will attack all of the saints with great determination.

One reason the false church will begin to attack all believers is because by that time the true church's leadership will be almost indistinguishable from the general body of believers. This is not because there are few leaders, but because so many will have matured and begun walking in leadership. This will be the result of a fundemental departure from traditional ministry development geared towards raising up professionals, to that which truly equips all of the saints to do the work of service.

The institutional churches will ultimately become the

greatest opposers of true believers, exceeding even the most anti-Christian governments, cults and religions. Every Christian that is in the institutional church will have to choose between their denomination and the Lord. This is nothing new; it has been this way with every new revival or restoration of truth. It will be more climactic during this time because the harvest that is the end of the age is the reaping of everything which has been sown, both the good and the evil. This is to be the ultimate clash between light and the darkness. The best and the worst of all ages will be standing eyeball to eyeball.

The False Church

Leading up to this there will be a great political union of almost every major denomination. Some of their priestly orders will be professionally trained to incite riots against believers, and to manipulate governments into arresting and executing them. This will not last long because the great mass of peoples will turn in rage against this institution as all of the wrath which they poured out is multiplied back to them. This is all working for the Lord's purposes, separating the tares from the wheat so that they can be destroyed without hurting the wheat.

We must heed a warning at this point. The Lord said to beware of the LEAVEN of the Pharisees; He did not say to beware of the Pharisees themselves. High churchmen are not our enemies; we do not war against flesh and blood, but against principalities and powers in the heavenly places. There are many "non-denominational churches which are as sectarian as any denominational church. Likewise, there are some denominational churches in which there seems to be little or no sectarian spirit. We must stop judging each other after the flesh, we must also stop judging congregations, movements, or ministries by externals.

Many of those who attack and kill believers will think they are doing God a favor, just as some of those did who carried out the Inquisitions. As the Lord Himself declared, as well as the first martyr after Him, we need to pray for the Father to forgive them because THEY REALLY DO NOT KNOW WHAT THEY ARE DOING. The Lord died for them too and wants to pluck as many of them from the fire of destruction as possible. The enemy's greatest victory is to seduce a chosen vessel of the Lord. Our greatest victory is to convert a chosen vessel of the enemy, and we are going to have more and greater victories in this than will the enemy.

When the church goes on the offensive against the enemy's strongholds, it will not be done by returning slander, or in the spirit of retaliation. The offensive strategy of the Lord is to bring conversion and release to the captives through the Truth Who sets all men free. We must return good for evil, praying for and witnessing to our enemies of the kindness of God that calls men to repentence.

Every Christian is called to be a martyr whether it becomes a literal death or not. We are called to die daily. If we have truly been buried with Him in baptism then we are dead to the world. What can the world do to a dead man? It is impossible for a dead man to be offended, feel rejected, or to fear death. This must become a reality to us in the days to come. When we perceive the riches of Christ we will call those blessed who go on to be with Him in fullness. We will understand why "Precious in the sight of the Lord is the death of His godly ones." (PS. 116:15).

The Lord has swallowed up death in victory. It has no more sting. This reality will give rise in the church to a boldness and straightforwardness about the gospel which has rarely been seen during the gospel age. This boldness will be in striking contrast to the paranoia gripping the earth. A revelation on baptism and martyrdom is coming that will establish in believers a peace that defies all human reasonings. The death that does work in the church will result in an unprecedented outpouring of life and freedom to the world. We are here and have been called by God for this purpose.

As this day of judgement unfolds, the scriptures will have increasingly real and immediate fulfillment. Those who seek to save their lives WILL lose them. Those who lay down their lives for the Lord's sake WILL find life that transcends their greatest expectations. Stephen was so consumed with the glory of the Lord that the stones which were meant to kill him could not even distract him. In the same way the glory of the Lord will be so great in these days that life and death on this earth will hold little significance for the saints. We WILL trust the Lord with our lives, the lives of our families, friends, and fellow members of the body of Christ.

In the future life will become very cheap throughout the world. Because of plagues, wars, riots and natural disasters, death will be witnessed almost daily by everyone. Burial will become as big a problem for some localities as waste removal, with fleets of trucks and armies of workers committed to the single task of carrying off the dead. Police will pay only casual attention to murders and other violent crimes taking place right in front of them. Ultimately, control will be completely lost by governments of the populations. For a time governments will be little more than criminal gangs who have banded together for the sake of plundering the people and protecting their own interests.

As this confusion and darkness increases the peace and vision of purpose displayed by the saints will be a marvel to the world. Many saints will be killed by the authorities and mobs. Others will disperse even the largest riots by simply standing in their way and praying for the Lord's peace to calm the storm. Some will approach government compounds and forts individually, and by the word of the Lord command them to disband, which they will do immediately. Companies of troops will bow to the Lord after attacking saints who stop their bullets and walk through their flame throwers. Others will believe because of the grace and honor with which the saints die. For the faithful, the laying down of this life for their Lord will be their greatest honor, and those who pass from this earth will not be mourned, but celebrated.

Islamic terrorists will have permeated the West with teams who have targeted Christian organizations and leaders. This is in preparation for an Islamic assault upon the entire world. They will have compiled computer data on almost every Christian leader who has any kind of extra-local influence (i.e. newsletters, a T.V. or radio outreach, etc.). Their main target for attacks will be denominations and institutions which they view as corrupt and satanic. They will seldom interfere with the actual harvest or the true church. Some will even closely identify with the radical lifestyle and belief of the saints, resulting in their conversion.

As the harvest begins to affect Islamic countries some will vehemently resisit it, but in general the harvest will reap many from among Islam. Egypt will be almost entirely won to the Lord; her devotion and willingness to sacrifice for His purposes will be so great she will actually be called "the alter of the Lord." Great apostles and prophets will come out of Islamic countries. These will rejoice greatly in the truth that sets them free, preaching the gospel with a commitment and abandon which will inspire the entire body of Christ.

CHAPTER 6

THE CHURCH AND ISRAEL

There will be a time of increasing controversy in the church about the place of Israel and Jews in the plan of God. This contention will polarize much of the church into extreme positions. These positions will basically consist of those who see only the natural Jew and the nation of Israel in God's purpose to close the age and bring in the end time harvest, and those who will see only spiritual Israel, the church which is composed of those who are Jews after the spirit, as having a purpose in the plan of God for this day. The enemy will try to make it one of the most devisive questions confronting the last day church. Satan is not targeting this just because it is convenient, but because the church's proper understanding of this issue will be essential if she is to fully accomplish her end time mandate.

Satan has historically caused such a controversy before the restoration of every important truth to the church. Ultimately this contention will result in a more clear revelation to the whole Body of Christ on this important and timely truth. As with most controversies, there is truth on both sides. This is not an attempt to resolve a contention which is yet in the future for most of the church, but simply to lay out the prophetic scenerio of what is to come. We must not be ignorant of the enemy's schemes or the Lord's purposes in this matter.

For almost two milleniums God's purposes were centralized in His dealings with the Jews. Then for almost two milleniums His purpose was concentrated with the church, which is spiritual Israel. Now, at the end of the age, there is to be a joining of the two into one, through Jesus, in such a way that it will be the crowning glory of the Lord's entire testimony of redemption. This is the grafting back in of the "natural branches" of which Paul prophesied in his letter to the Romans. As he so accurately foresaw, if the rejection of the Jews resulted in reconciliation for the world, then their reacceptance will actually bring life from the dead, the beginning of the resurrection (ROM. 11:15). Through this union of Israel and the church, in Jesus, there will be a release of life and power unequaled on earth since the Spirit first moved on the formless void.

The natural seed of Abraham, or the Jew according to the flesh, and the spiritual seed, the Jew according to the spirit, or heart, both represent God's purposes in redemption. The church has been torn between the two opinions of those who see the promises in heaven and those who see the redemption and restoration of the earth. Both of these positions are verified in scripture, and both have truth. The apparent inconsistances cannot be resolved, by God's design, until we come to understand what Paul called "the mystery" of the joining together of Jew and Gentile into one, as he related to the Romans and the Ephesians. Only when we understand this joining will we comprehend God's purpose of both the heavenly calling and the redemption of the earth.

This revelation of the two opposing seeds being grafted into one represents such a glory of the character of God that it will literally release the Holy Spirit in the earth with such power and life that the resurrection will begin. This also marks the end of the times of the Gentiles and the beginning of the times of the Jews and Gentiles together. This represents the end of antithesis in the creation, and the beginning of a synthesis of all that has fallen back into union with the purposes God. The whole creation, that which is spirit and that which is natural, will be enraptured in the love and devotion between the Father and the Son until the barriers between the natural and spiritual are removed, beginning a free interchange between the heavens and the earth. Neither will be changed in nature; that is, that which is spirit will not become natural and vice versa, but the interchange will be free and unhindered.

The above is a scenerio of "the restoration of all things about which God spoke by the mouth of His holy prophets from ancient time" (ACTS 3:21). This revelation has not yet be fully given because it is not quite the time. Many are starting to get parts of this revelation, and often carrying them to extremes which is often the result when we become dogmatic with only part of the truth.

Because of the ultimate significance of this truth to God's purposes, Satan will soon be releasing every demon in hell to divide the church over these issues and to bring enmity between Christians and Jews. What took place in Nazi Germany will not compare to the anti-semitic and anti-Christ spirit soon to sweep the earth. The anti-semitic spirit will rise in the church and the anti-Christ spirit will rage among Jews. Both spirits will dominate the rest of the world until they promote a major attack by every religion and philosophy on earth. In time there will hardly be a person in the world not touched by the resulting conflict. Just as the Jews became the most vehement enemies of the gospel at the end of their age, many misguided Christian leaders will become enemies of this great purpose of God at the end of the times of the Gentiles. Like their Jewish counterparts in the first century, those who are so deluded will consider themselves the protectors of the true faith.

Middle East War

A conflict in the Middle East will result in Israel utterly destroying Damascus in such a way the the entire world will be enraged at them. Problems then sweeping the world will be blamed on Jews who will have been holding key economic and political positions, which will seemingly indicate a conspiracy. Even the U.S. will wash its hands of Israel and participate in the new holocaust. Jews will be killed and driven out of every nation on earth.

During this time true believers around the world will rise to give Jews aid and shelter, igniting even greater wrath against Christians. That Jews and Christians find themselves together in this persecution is by Divine design. Twenty centuries of persecution and reproach has prepared the Jews for the TRUE gospel. Christians who have remained faithful through these times will have the true gospel.

Christians who shelter the persecuted Jews will not give in to human, unsanctified sympathy for the Jew's troubles. These believers will earnestly, and with such authority and clarity, confront them with the gospel, that it will begin "grafting" Israel back into the true faith of Abraham. They will meet and believe their Messiah. Their two thousand years of persecution at the hands of false Christianity will help them understand true Christianity, history and the unfolding plan of God like few others can.

During this same period, the Soviets, in league with Iran and other Islamic nations, will march against Israel with world public opinion on their side. No other country will help Israel but the assault will be stopped by an earthquake and great storms. This will so undeniably be an act of God that it will also stop the world-wide assault against Christians as well, fanning the flames of revival until believers will have to hide in order to sleep because of the multitudes seeking salvation.

This will be the most glorious advance that the church is to make before the return of the Lord. The Jews and the gentiles were meant to be one loaf (see EPH.2:14-18). The plan will not be complete until they are joined, in Christ. When the times of the gentiles end it is the beginning of the times of the Jews and the Gentiles, which will not be completed until there is neither Jew nor Gentile, but all nations have come together to be one in Christ.

These are major signs of the times: When anti-semitism begins to dominate the church and the world we are entering the "deep darkness" which will cover the earth (IS.60:1-2). It is always darkest before the dawn; when the two olive trees are grafted into one, the most terrible darkness in all of history will then begin fading into light.

It has often been because of the weakness of the message they preach that some have promulgated the false notion that the Jews have a special and acceptable position with God outside of Christ. This is a delusion we must dispel. It is a misguided sentimentality that compels the church to send money or other aid to Israel so that she can buy rockets or build cities. This does not bless Israel, it works to strengthen her will to resist the gospel, which she will do as long as she can stand on her own strength.

As Paul made clear, "from the standpoint of gospel they (the Jews) are enemies FOR YOUR SAKE" (ROM.11:28). It is important that the church understand that the Jews are enemies of the gospel, but FOR OUR SAKE. The Lord has made the Jew the greatest test of whether or not we are preaching a true gospel. Only the true gospel will move the Jews to jealousy as it was commissioned to do. The ability of our gospel to move the Jew is the acid test meant to determine if we are preaching the undiluted truth. This was a reason for their dispersion to all nations. There is hardly a place we can go with the gospel that they will not be a thorn in our flesh, to challenge and buffet us, but force us to be true. Though it is important to win the weak and down-trodden, it is not difficult to get a decision out of a drunk in the gutter, the homeless, or the spent and disoriented prosti-tute. If you want to find out if you have the goods or not, confront the Jew with your gospel. The Lord commanded the gospel to be preached to the Jew first, not because of favorit-ism, but because of the special challenge they present which is meant to make us dig deeper into the wells of salvation.

When the apostolic ministry has been fully restored, so will the apostolic message concerning Israel: the grafting back in of the Jew and Israel's role in God's plan for this day. With this revelation an illumination will also come on His plan for the church which transcends that which is presently under-stood. The purposes of the earthly and heavenly seeds of Abraham have set them on a collision course for this time so that neither can fulfill their calling without the other. This revelation will meet great opposition for a time, but at the right time the scales will fall from the eyes of the church on this issue. But this will remain a mystery, and a controversy until that time. It is the consummation of the age when spiritual Israel and "natural" Israel become ONE IN CHRIST.

The Lord promised Abraham that those who blessed him and his seed would be blessed, and those who cursed him would be cursed. This applies to both the spiritual and the earthly seed. Historically it seems that those who blessed the natural seed received natural blessings, and those who blessed the spiritual seed received spiritual blessings. As a testimony that the purpose of God is now approaching the synthesis of the two seeds, those who bless natural Israel (the Jews) will be receiving spiritual blessings and those who bless spiritual Israel (the church) will be receiving natural blessings. Because

109

of one righteous act by Harry S. Truman, when he recognized the new state of Israel against the counsel of almost everyone in our government, as well as world opinion, his home town of Kansas City will be a center of revival in the U.S. during the last days, and be a blessing to many other nations. As a legacy to Anwar Sadat, who likewise recognized Israel against great opposition, the entire nation of Egypt will call on the name of Jesus and water the deserts of the earth with the gospel.

As the day draws closer there will be an increasing release in the spirit when we recognize God's purpose with Israel. Likewise, there will be an increasing release of the spirit in Israel as she begins to recognize God's purpose in the church. There will also be an increasingly swift judgement against those who become arrogant toward the natural branches, just as the apostle warned (ROM.11:18-22). This must be so because of the significance of what will result when the two olive trees become one. The joining of the natural and heavenly seeds will ultimately result in the free interchange between the heavens and the earth, making it possible for God Who is Spirit to dwell on earth among men, in His fulness.

CHAPTER 7

THE TITANIC AND THE STOCK MARKET

To interpret current events in the light of Divine purpose is a primary function of the prophets. They must see the relationships between events in conjunction with His works and His message. God's prophets do not just foretell or predict, but much of their ministry is devoted to the explanation of signs and messages. There are extraordinary events taking place today which do have a message for those who will hear. Two of these recent, significant events are the discovery of the Titanic on the bottom of the North Atlantic, and the Stock Market Crash of 1987--and these are related.

When built, the Titanic was a symbol of the opulence and seeming invincibility the British Empire presumed in those days. The Titanic reflected that period's extravagance, and arrogance, as well as the belief that nothing could sink their expanding world economy and dominion. This attitude is in contrast to God's wisdom which warns: "Pride goes before destruction and a haughty spirit before stumbling" (Prov. 16:18). But few considered His wisdom. No one dreamed that in just two short years the whole world would be in the flames of war, and that their invincible empire was about to hit an iceberg that would ultimately send them to the same ash heap of history where every one of man's previous empires had gone.

Many in the British clergy encouraged the arrogance of the empire. They preached a conservative patriotism because they saw the empire as the only true protector of the faith and promulgator of the gospel. Their missionaries circled the globe to convert natives in the colonies. Their spiritual heritage was rich; British subjects who refused to compromise their convictions impacted the world with revival and reformation. They also gave the world one of its greatest spiritual gifts--the King James Version of the Bible. They could foresee no other country in the world carrying the mantle of spiritual authority as she had.

But by the turn of the century Britain had reached her limits and was beginning to regress. She was resting more on what she had accomplished than on what was left to do. Pride had replaced vision. When this happens the end is always near. The Titanic was a message the Lord gave Britain to call her to repentance; repentance that would enable her to continue leading the world toward the fulfillment of His purposes, and would give her the opportunity to reach greater spiritual heights. She did not listen. Now she is firmly entrenched in tradition, her greatness in the past, the mantle given to another.

Just as the Lord used the British Empire for a period, He has used the United States in a great and wonderful way. We have possibly surpassed the British in preaching the gospel, we were used to aid in the establishment of Israel, and as the primary hedge against the communist plague. By giving purpose and meaning to the value of the individual, America rose to be the greatest nation in history. When we had the power to dominate the world and dictate policy as the lone possessor of nuclear weapons, our esteem for liberty and free determination would hardly consider it. We were a nation of pioneers, more interested in going somewhere new or making something new. The apostle exhorted us to give honor to whom honor is due; we should give a great deal to our ancestors who risked their lives, their fortunes and their sacred honor so that we could live in a land of liberty. Now, as painful as it is to see, the handwriting is on our wall. The most destructive thing that can happen to a great nation has happened to us--our vision has been turned to pride. We have begun to rest more on what has been done than pressing on towards what is left to do.

Paul warned the Gentiles who have been grafted into the vine because of the Jew's hardness of heart, that they too could be quickly removed by their own pride. In the same way, pride can remove a nation from its position in God's purposes. He is able to raise up even the most insignificant nation to take its place. He does not need the United States; we need Him. The sinking of the Titanic was a warning to the empire to repent of its arrogance, signifying that nothing man can build is invincible. Her recent discovery on the bottom of the North Atlantic is a timely reminder of just how foolish some of our present arrogance will prove to be if we do not repent of it. In the same way the space shuttle catastrophe was a warning to the United States. The glory of this nation of technological wonders was rising to the heavens one minute, and the next she was gone, exactly like the Biblical admonition:

"And I will grant wonders in the sky above, And signs on the earth beneath, Blood, and fire, and vapor of smoke" (Acts 2:19).

The nation was shocked and horrified by the blood, the fire, and vapor of smoke the Challenger burned in our hearts that day--but did we get the message? The Lord did not blow up the Challenger; it was our pride that caused it. Pride breeds carelessness. Without repentance this nation can evaporate into a few tiny little fragments just as quickly as the shuttle did. Economically we are primed for just such a disaster.

Is there no hope for the United States? Yes, if there is repentance. With every prophet and warning sent by the Lord there is an appeal for repentance. The judgments foretold come to pass only if we refuse to hear and turn from our wicked ways. There were many prophecies given in the 1970's about the impending judgment of God on America. Then there was a measure of repentance which delayed the judgment, just as the Lord did on occasion for Biblical nations. Do not think because the judgments did not come to pass that the prophecies were not from the Lord; they accomplished the necessary repentance and the Lord gave more time.

It does not take much repentance for the Lord to relent of His intended judgment. When Abraham asked if He would spare Sodom for just ten righteous men He said that He would. The repentance experienced by the U.S. seemed hardly measurable to many prophets, but it was enough for the Lord to give us longer. He tends to be far more gracious than His prophets. If there is a measure of turning from the evil that would bring His judgment, and the Lord relents again for a period of time, are we going to be like Jonah and mourn because the Lord did not bring down His fire? Are we going to be discouraged and refuse to keep prophesying? No. Let us speak His words with boldness while praying for the people to hear and repent. A single soul is worth more than our pride; how much more an entire nation?

We must pray for repentance that these things will not have to come to pass now, but we know by the Biblical prophecies that they eventually will. It seems this may well be the time. The Lord knows the end from the beginning and He knows there will be a time when there will be no repentance. Many are saying today, "We've heard that all before and nothing happened." Few understand why nothing happened. The scriptures are clear that times of trouble will come upon the world; we should always be ready. Let us pray for repentance, but prepare for the tribulations. If it is time we know the kingdom is that much closer, so we have cause for rejoicing either way. But do not be like the foolish virgins who decided to sleep because the Lord seemed to delay His coming. If He gives us another year or fifty, let us use the time wisely.

Pride Is A Time Bomb

Let us understand, the Lord did not sink the Titanic--pride sank her. Because they didn't think she could sink they sailed boldly into dangerous waters with reckless abandon. This "unsinkable" pride of the Empire proved to be incredibly fragile, just like the Empire itself, just like every empire.

In relation to the present world economy it has been repeated often, and believed by most, that what happened in 1929 could never happen again. It is said that there are too many safeguards such as a stronger Federal Reserve, higher margin requirements for speculators and institutions, FDIC, FSLIC, SIPC, etc... Do not believe it. We are now more vulnerable to a world-wide economic catastrophe than at any time in history, and we are sailing along merrily in the most treacherous of seas.

Without repentance and Divine intervention the U.S. is on a course leading to almost total economic collapse. This catastrophe will send the entire world economy staggering to the point where there will not be a secure economy again during this age. Erosion will continue, with but brief reprieves, until the entire world economic system has unraveled. At this time the lifestyle of even some of the more prosperous nations will then be more like the 19th century than the 20th.

The Fed, FDIC and all of the other safeguards are lifeboats that may save a few, but they are completely inadequate for the voyage we're on. The owners of Titanic felt that having even half the lifeboats a ship her size should have carried was superfluous. Today's leaders are sailing with the same disdain for reason while touting their ingenuity in designing a ship they think cannot sink. In October of 1987 we hit an iceberg and we are about to see just how unsinkable this ship is.

Students of history marvel at the repetitious cycles of human mistakes. Few have been able to break out of these cycles. Few have been wise enough to see anything but what they wanted to see in the trends and events taking place around them. This has also been the case with many who were called as prophets to warn the world and the church. As it was with the Biblical seers, those calling for repentance will be lonely voices. The majority who claim to be messengers will usually be found preaching prosperity and peace; the majority have always been more concerned about their acceptance than the truth of the message.

Those in authority, by the nature of their power, feel compelled to put the best face on problems. Only the most courageous leaders have been able to hear the warnings and take action. Empire after empire, nation after nation, organizations, companies, churches and families, continue to fail because their leaders refuse to face the problems until they are beyond control.

It is amazing how the reactions of the politicians and experts after the Stock Market crash of October 1987 echoed the voices of October 1929. In some cases you wondered if they were reading from a history book! After the 1929 crash, the first response of the politicians was to point out the "underlying health of the economy". Christmas sales that year were as brisk as ever. The crash was soon almost forgotten, remembered as a curiosity more than anything else. The market even began to rise again and continued for almost three years, until June of 1932 when the Depression really began.

Even though it was under the surface for awhile, the economy began unraveling in 1929 with the crash; the ship then began taking on water. Pressure rose for the government to do something. As much as they tried to do what Wall Street demanded, their efforts only exacerbated the problem. As it turned out, the underlying health of the economy was far more fragile than anyone had foreseen.

When the Titanic hit the iceberg there was a disconcerting jolt. Just about everyone noticed it, but after a couple of minutes the party continued. No one could imagine that in just two hours most of them would be on the bottom. The ship was so big, and all of the experts said it was unsinkable. As well as everything seems at present it is almost incomprehensible that catastrophe may be upon us. The Lord Jesus and Paul both warned us it would be just this way when it happens.

> For as in those days which were before the flood they were eating and drinking, they were marrying and giving in marriage, until the day that Noah entered the ark... and they did not understand until the flood came and took them all away (Matt.24:38-39).

> While they are saying, "Peace and safety!" then destruction will come upon them suddenly ...... But you, brethren, are not in darkness, that the day should overtake you like a thief (I Thes.5:3).

The Stock Market is usually a thermometer which continually takes the temperature of business. It reflects the value the world puts on the economy. Occasionally it becomes a thermostat, setting the direction and pace of business. When that happens it is usually catastrophic. Not since 1929 has this change come with the force it did in October 1987. It is no longer just measuring the economy, it is now dictating policy. The only time it can do this is when extreme damage control measures are required.

A good portion of the world's investors woke up on Black Monday gripped with panic. There was little difference between that day and any other we'd had recently. As Roger Smith, the Chairman of General Motors, stated when asked about the recent turmoil on Wall Street: "We didn't just have a tummy ache here in our country; we had a genuine, certified heart attack! If you don't recognize it as a heart attack, and if you don't get on that diet and start doing your exercise, you can have another one and it could be terminal."

Roger Smith was right. Black Monday was a bonafide heart attack for the world's economy because the U.S. is the heart of the world economy. It was not a fatal heart attack; it was a warning that there are very serious problems. If these are not dealt with the next one could well be the big one. So far they have not been dealt with; they have not even been addressed.

Even though it was a deadly presumption for the engineers to proclaim the ship unsinkable, the complacency of the leadership on the Titanic was the single greatest reason for the disaster. Captain Smith and his crew received numerous warnings about the ice field which lay directly across their path, and they did not even slow down! Even if it were unsinkable, to hit an iceberg head on would almost certainly cause great damage and loss of life. The only possible reason for Smith's proceeding with such disdain for the danger is an incredible false sense of security. When one looks at the course of Western economic policy for the last couple of decades, like Smith, one wonders what our leaders could possibly be thinking, and how have we survived a catastrophe this long? The only answer is that the Lord really does have His angels holding back the four winds of the earth until He completes the work in His bondservants (Rev.7:1).

The Bible warned that it would be like this in these days. It does not warn us just so that we can know our doom, but so we can be prepared and take action. We need not fear anything if we are abiding in Christ, because in Him we are delivered from the judgments of God. We are here because the greatest move of God in history is also about to take place, and we are a part of that move.

It does appear we have come to the time of the greatest troubles ever known, but these are also birth pangs for the coming of a new age, one in which our King will reign. He exhorted us to know the signs of the times and to be prepared. This is not just to save ourselves, but others as well. There is much for us to do, but we will not be able to save others if we are drowning ourselves.

In the near future devastating economic problems will be sweeping the world in waves. Great countries and societies will begin collapsing. Like the passengers on the Titanic, the water will lap at our ankles, then our knees; then there will be a mad rush to the highest part on the ship. It will all be in vain, because the whole ship IS going to sink. The entire world system is near its end. But we don't have to go down with this ship, because we don't have to be on it. The Lord is now calling us to board the ONLY ship which cannot sink, the kingdom of God.

When the lifeboats began leaving the Titanic the first ones were only partially filled because most refused to leave the warmth of the ship. They just did not believe it was really sinking. By the time it was obvious that it was sinking the boats were gone. The Lord is NOW loading His Lifeboat. "TODAY if you hear His voice, do not harden you hearts" (Heb.4:7). "Therefore, let everyone who is godly pray to Thee in a time when Thou mayest be found; surely in a flood of great waters they shall not reach Him." (Psalm 32:6).

The Ark

So what do we do? We must earnestly seek the Lord. I do not mean seek Him for instructions as to what we should do--seek Him because HE IS what we should do. He is the Ark of God in Whom we will be delivered from every flood. He Himself bore the curse of our sin, absorbed the judgment that was ours. If we are abiding in Him we do not have to fear the judgment against sin. This does not mean that we will not be here, or will not have to endure tribulation. It does mean that even if we are called to walk through the fire, it will not burn us; the floods may come, but our house will be built upon a rock which can sustain them.

For years doctrines have been preached which have lulled much of the church into a deep sleep. They did this with assurances that those in Christ would not have to go through tribulation. This is contrary to the testimony of Scripture and it is quite amazing how so many would believe it without the presence of a strong delusion. Some hold this doctrine to the degree that they believe anyone who preaches anything contrary is a false teacher, or prophet. Let us consider, would it be better to be prepared and not have to go through tribulation, or not to be prepared and have to go through it? As Corrie ten Boom once stated: "I have been in countries where the saints are already suffering terrible persecution. In China the Christians were told, 'Don't worry, before the tribulation comes, you will be translated--raptured.' Then came a terrible persecution. Millions of Christians were tortured to death. Later I heard a Bishop from China say, sadly, 'We have failed. We should have made the people strong for persecution rather than telling them Jesus would come first.' Turning to me he said, 'You will have time. Tell the people how to be strong in times of persecution, how to stand when the tribulation comes--to stand and not faint.

The Lord exhorted us over and over to be ready and watching, and always to be prepared. This does not necessarily imply that we should be storing food and bullets, but that we should be ready to take action in season and out of season. We cannot be like the crew of the Titanic who did not think that anything adverse could happen to them, because that is precisely when we are the most vulnerable. There is no scripture which says we will be raptured before tribulation. There obviously is a time when those who are in Christ will be changed, but nowhere does is indicate when. Many have based their entire hope on the conjecture of a few men, when the whole Bible is a testimony of God's deliverance and victory THROUGH tribulation. The church in the last day will go through the worst tribulation in history, and will prevail against it, leading the rest of creation out of its bondage.

"All things work together for good for those who love God and are called according to His purpose" (Rom.8:28), EVEN THE GREAT TRIBULATION. This will be the church's finest hour, her greatest victory. "In all things we OVER-WHELMINGLY conquer through Him" (Rom.8:37).

"He ALWAYS leads us in His triumph in Christ" (II Cor.

119

2:14). This is not the time to run, it is time for the church to draw her spiritual sword and attack. The doctrine of the rapture was a great and effective ruse of the enemy to implant in the church a retreat mentality, but it will not succeed. Already this yoke has been cast off by the majority in the advancing church, and it will soon be cast off by all. Instead, the church will not even want to miss this time. It will bring the greatest battle between light and darkness, and the light is going to prevail.

If we have the true fear of the Lord we need not fear anything else. The Lord clearly told us how we can build our houses on the rock that would endure the storm (Matt.7: 24-27). There are only two requirements--to hear His words, and then to act on them, BUT WE MUST DO BOTH, and we must do them now. We cannot wait until the floods come. The winds are presently being restrained by the angels of the Lord, but they will not be held back forever. We must use this time wisely.

The world systems and governments are already sinking. In scripture, mountains are often symbolic of governments and the sea speaks of the mass of humanity (Rev.17:15, Is.17: 12-13). As it says in Psalm 46:2, the mountains will slip into the sea, but we shall not fear. In the days to come all governments will be melting like wax (PS.97:5) and for a time the shifting seas which are in great confusion and turmoil will begin washing them away. However, God's government will not be moved, but will grow stronger in the earth as all others dissolve. But we must understand one thing: His kingdom is not OF this world, it is very different than the governments of this world. There is some confusion over this in the church today, but it will be clarified in due time. The coming of the kingdom of God is an irresistible force. Those who are sincerely seeking Him and His glory, not just their own position and recognition, will be a part of that force.

The doctrine of the kingdom is yet to be preached. The doctrine of salvation has gone into most of the world, but not the gospel of the kingdom. There are many preaching "a" doctrine of the kingdom, but we are yet to hear "THE" message of the kingdom. The coming of the kingdom is going to be far more subtle than we have been led to believe. As

Jesus warned the Pharisees, who had very carefully laid out their doctrines on the coming kingdom of the Messiah: "The kingdom of God cometh not with observation" (Luke 17:20).

Though we may not yet know exactly how it is coming to the earth, we know that it is, and we know how to prepare for it. We can live in the kingdom now by abiding in the King. If we are abiding in Him we will be prepared for every circumstance, and we will be empowered to take advantage of them for His glory.

Three Kinds Of Leadership

The tragedy of the Titanic brought to light a striking revelation of three kinds of leadership, all three of which can be seen in the world and the church, today.

The first type can be seen in Captain Smith and the crew of the Titanic. These were the best from the British merchant fleet. There possibly was not a more intelligent, experienced or knowledgeable sea captain in the Empire than Smith. Combine this with his record of never having had a single accident at sea, and we have what appeared to be an unsinkable crew with an unsinkable ship. Actually, these characteristics are most probably the greatest contributing factor to the doom of this ship. These all fed the pride, which feeds carelessness, which sooner or later usually leads to tragedy.

The Titanic's crew had never held a proper lifeboat drill. They did not have a plan for the orderly movement of passengers to the boats, and most of the crew did not even know how to lower them. Everything had to be planned and learned while the ship was sinking under their feet. This obviously contributed to a much greater loss of life than was necessary. Many boats were lowered only partially full, one with only twelve people, while hundreds of passengers were held below decks by the crew. The entire ship had been caught off guard by the events of that fateful night, and they paid dearly for it. Will we be caught in the same position? If we are we will pay just as dearly. But we don't have to be surprised. The Lord exhorted us to know the signs of the times, and not to sleep on our watch. Prophets throughout the land are now calling for PREPARATION; the Lord is giving us signs in the heavens and on the earth. He is sounding His trumpet, and we must hear it.

As discussed earlier, every great man of God was only successful after passing through the fires of failure and defeat. Though an unpopular teaching, it is the continuous testimony of scripture. As so many of the elders and fathers of the faith would not trust a man until he had his "limp", we would be wise, and far more safe, if we followed their example. The twentieth century prophet, Alexandr Solzhenitsyn, declared, "Does not even biology itself teach us that perpetual well being is not good for any living thing?" Perpetual well being can open doors to a most dangerous enemy--complacency. What else can explain how the Titanic crew could receive six warnings that there were deadly icebergs directly in their path, and yet they did not even slow down!

The Bible is most candid about the failures and mistakes of even its greatest heros. This is a message in itself. We must "take heed when we think we stand, lest we fall." Even the greatest in the faith had defeats and failures. Even the apostle Paul could be "foiled by Satan." When I hear the testimonies of individuals and churches which have never been deceived, or made great mistakes, it does not build my confidence in them, it detracts from it. If one hasn't been wounded he has not yet been in this fight, and he will be prone, not just to get wounded, but to get killed, as did the crew of the Titanic.

There were two other ships which played a significant role in the drama of the Titanic disaster: the Californian and the Carpathia. The captains of these ships remarkably parallel the two other prevailing types of leadership found today.

The Californian had a captain who had obviously learned something from his years of successes and failures. He was reserved and cautious, but overly cautious. The realities of life may cause us to react this way if we allow the fear of more failure to sow in us a perpetual hesitancy. Becoming overly cautious can be just as deadly as being overly confident, as it was in this case.

When Captain Lord of the Californian heard about the ice in his path, he slowed down. When he saw the ice he ordered the ship stopped and waited for daylight. His wireless (radio) operator began warning the other ships in the area of the danger. At 7:30 p.m. her warning was received and logged by the Titanic.

The usually stormy North Atlantic was incredibly calm that night. More than one officer remarked that they had never seen the sea so tranquil. First officer Lightoller of the Titanic made this observation at the inquiry when he declared that "everything was against us." This tranquility must have overcome the crew of the Californian as well. Her bridge watch saw the Titanic approaching just a few miles away; then saw her stop dead in the water. At first they probably thought she was taking the same precautions for the ice which they had taken. Then she started firing rockets into the air every few minutes--always a distress signal at sea. They rationalized this, remarking that it must be a signal meant for another company ship which they could not see. They did not even bother to wake the wireless operator to see if he could contact the ship. Then they watched her disappear, telling each other that she was sailing away when she was actually slipping beneath the sea. Had they responded to the first distress signal the Californian may well have been able to save all of the lives that were lost.

The lackadaisical attitude of the Californian crew is beyond comprehension, just as is the attitude of the majority of the church today. When the final inquiry comes and the final story is told, we are going to marvel at how many were in a position to save life, but instead slept right through the night just as the captain of the Californian did, when he could have done so much. Rationalization is a popular shield for cowards. Were they so afraid of the ice that they decided to humor each other with such unbelievable reasons for not responding to the obvious emergency? Are we going to have to ask ourselves a similar question? As our world sinks into the deep are we going to sleep when we could be saving many, or are we going to rise up and take action?

REV.21:8 says, "the cowardly and unbelieving and abominable and murderers and immoral persons and sorcerers and idolaters and liars, their part will be in the lake that burns with fire and brimstone, which is the second death." Cowards are here lumped together with the murderers because their actions often lead to the death of others when they could have helped, just as it did for the people on the Titanic. As Christians we may hide and save our lives during times of trouble, but we may very well by this action be putting ourselves in the most terrible jeopardy for all eternity. If we cower and seek to save our lives, we will lose them just like the Lord warned. It is only by losing our own lives that we will find them. Cowards have no place in the kingdom of God. "Those who know their God will display strength and take action."

The third ship in the fateful drama of that night was the Carpathia, captained by Arthur H. Rostron. He was known for the ability to make quick decisions and to energize those who served under him. He is a wonderful example of the leadership the Lord is preparing for this day. Rostron was a pious man devoted to prayer. At 12:35 a.m. the Carpathia's wireless operator burst into his quarters to report that the Titanic had struck an iceberg. Rostron reacted in character; he immediately ordered the Carpathia turned around and full speed ahead, later asking the operator if he was sure about the report, a striking contrast to the reaction on the Californian.

Rostron then gave an incredible display of a truly prepared mind; he thought of everything and took care of every detail. He ordered the English doctor to the first class dining room, the Italian doctor to second class, the Hungarian to third class, along with every possible piece of equipment or supplies needed for the sick and wounded. He ordered different officers to different gangways, instructing them to get the names of survivors to send by wireless. They prepared block and lines with chair slings for the wounded. Bowlines were secured along the ships sides along with boat ropes and heaving lines for lifting people in chairs. All gangway doors were opened. He then directed specific officers to take charge of his present passengers and to see to their needs. All hands were to prepare coffee, soup and provisions. He then designated all officers cabin's, smoke rooms, library, etc., as accommodations for the survivors. Stewards were sent to reassure and explain to their own passengers the reason for the activity to help keep them calm.

Then Rostron turned to face the biggest problem of all, the ice. He was heading at full speed into the same field that had stopped the Titanic. To this courageous man reducing speed was out of the question, but he took every measure to reduce the risk to his own ship and passengers. He added a man to the crow's nest, put two more on the bow, one on each wing of the bridge, and he stayed there himself. His second officer, James Bisset, then noticed his captain taking one last measure which he considered the most important of all. He prayed.

At 2:45 a.m. Bisset saw the first iceberg. They steered around it and kept going. The next hour they dodged five more. At 4:00 a.m. they reached the Titanic's last called position and began picking up lifeboats. As the sun rose it revealed an astonishing sight; the sea was full of icebergs for as far as the eye could see in all directions. Even with all the lookouts, the Carpathia had passed numerous icebergs which they had not even seen. No one could imagine how they missed them all, except their pious captain.

The difficult rescue of the survivors was carried out with such order and discipline that peace reigned over all. The Carpathia's passengers caught the spirit of self-sacrifice from her crew. Her first class passengers gave their own quarters to survivors; others were pitching in to do all they could. On one of the darkest nights of tragedy ever experienced on the high seas, the Carpathia's captain, crew and passengers stand out as bright lights of courage and heroism. They are a demonstration of what the Lord has called us to be in the night of tragedy and loss that is now falling upon the earth. Let us not sleep as some did, or be fooled by the calmness of the sea. Let us be PREPARED!

Wars, Earthquakes, Famines And Plagues

We know from the testimony of scripture that the last days will be the greatest time of trouble the world has ever seen. A good portion of the loss and devastation will be the result of unpreparedness. Such peace and relative prosperity will preceed this time of trouble that almost the entire world will have been lulled into tranquility until evil is released like the springing of a great trap. Once the unraveling of these events begin they will accelerate with breathtaking speed. If we are not prepared before this flood begins it truly will be too late. Now is the time for us to put our houses in order.

As a jet pilot one of the first things I learned was to pay close attention to my engine instruments and know what they were indicating. Even if the particular systems were staying within their tolerances, certain trends could foretell serious problems. If there are erratic occilations, even though they stay within acceptable parameters, the engine may not just quit, it could very well explode! The political, economic and environmental instruments of the entire world are now wildly occilating, and they have long ago, and by a large margin, departed their safe parameters. The indicators are trying to warn us that this engine may not just gradually lose power when it decides to quit, but it may blow-up with terrible force.

In 1987 we had the greatest stock market crash in history, impacting every major market in the world overnight. The very next day we had the greatest market advance in history. In 1988 we had a presidential candidate with a seemingly insurmountable 17 point lead in opinion polls fall behind by 17 points in just a few weeks, never to recover. We have the leader of the first and most powerful communist country calling for democratic reform and a limited free market system, while other major policy changes are taking place in many other communist and Western nations. In 1988 we also had the most powerful hurricane in recorded history, the worst forest fires, one of the worst earthquakes, record low temperatures in the Atlantic, record high and low temperatures in a multitude of other regions throughout the world, with some breaking previous records by almost 15 degrees, setting high and low records in the same areas during the same seasons, record droughts and record rainfalls, even in the same regions. We have become almost desensitized by the fact that these records are now being set continually, and by increasing margins. Political, economic and environmental instruments are all wildly occilating AND departing their safe parameters. These trends are messages.

We are now entering a period when wars will increase and

then subside until there is almost total peace in the world. There will be some devastating attacks by the most cruel weapons, even nuclear exchanges but on a limited basis, and mostly between third world nations. More will perish by plagues and natural disasters than by wars during the period of this vision. The very foundations of civilization will shake and erode. Even the most stable governments will be collapsing, losing authority and control over their populations. Eventually it will be hard to find anyone with the courage to take authority. This will ultimately cause paranoia and anarchy to spread over the entire earth.

Devastating earthquakes will continue to increase in frequency. Some of the most deadly will strike areas that were previously considered safe from earthquakes. This will make them more deadly because earthquakes were not a consideration during construction planning. Also, with there being fewer faults in these areas to shift and absorb the energy, the shock waves will be transmitted over much greater distances while maintaining a high level of energy.

One of these killer quakes will hit the east coast of the U.S. with such force that it will be felt on the West Coast. Damage from this quake will extend west of the Mississippi River. An earthquake will devastate Florida and break it off from the mainland. The western coastline will be drastically changed by a major quake. In some areas the ocean will extend inland until it reaches what is now desert. Both Asia and southern Europe will be repeatedly hit by record breaking quakes, some of which will almost wipe out entire nations. One major nation in southern Europe will disappear except for a few small islands. Because of the destruction of powerplants and powerline systems, large sections of the most advanced and modern nations will be without electrical power for years. This will so drastically change the lifestyle of these areas that it will be more like the nineteenth century than the twentieth.

The spread of AIDS will continue until it becomes one of the greatest killers of all time. The nature of this virus will change so that it will be transmitted through casual contact, mosquitoes, and even food.

Huge mobs will attack everything in their path. The infrastructure of the great denominational churches and large visible ministries will be one of their primary targets and will vanish almost overnight. Pagan religions, cults and witchcraft will spread like plagues but these will also become targets of the mobs. By this time governments will have broken down to the point where lynchings and mass executions perpetrated by these mobs are overlooked by the authorities.

Light Is Stronger Than Darkness

Fear and deep darkness will cover the earth, but this will accentuate the glory which is appearing upon the saints. Masses of people will be streaming to the Lord, the inflow so great in places that very young Christians will be pastoring large bodies of believers. Arenas and stadiums will overflow nightly as the believers come together to hear the apostles and teachers.

At this time few congregations will remain separate or individual entities. Many elders and pastors may be stationary but groups they oversee will be constantly changing. Some of these will be moving on because of persecution and others because the Lord will scatter them to carry His message abroad like seed.

Near the end (of the vision) the body of Christ is like a great flowing river sweeping about as freely as the wind. One day there will be meetings in a public auditorium or stadium, the next day in a park, and there will be saints meeting continually from house to house. Great meetings that stir entire cities will happen spontaneously. Extraordinary miracles will be common while those considered great today will be performed almost without notice by young believers. Angelic appearances will be common to the saints and a visible glory of the Lord will appear upon some for extended periods of time as power flows through them.

There will be no plague, disease, or physical condition, including lost limbs, AIDS, poison gas, or radiation, which will resist the healing and miracle gifts working in the saints during this time. Food will be multiplied day after day where there is no other provision. At times the Lord will provide abundant supplies from heaven like He did with Israel in the wilderness. Apostles and prophets will stand up to bless fields and cities in the name of the Lord and to remove every trace of radiation from them.

Conferences of apostles, prophets, pastors, elders, etc.. will be called and used greatly by the Lord, but without denominating and separating from the rest of the body. Their unity will be in Jesus and He alone will be the Head of His church. Eventually, the Lord's presence will be so great during this revival that, like the twenty-four elders in Revelation, all crowns will be cast at His feet and spiritual presumption will be unthinkable. Those in leadership will be the most humble of all. Those who presume leadership without calling will be apparent to all. The leaders of this move will be true servants, not interested in reputation or position. Their humility will open them to become channels for wave after wave of living water.

This harvest will be so great that no one will look back at the early church as a standard; all will be saying that the Lord has certainly saved His best wine for last. The early church was a firstfruits offering, truly this will be a harvest! It was said of the Apostle Paul that he was turning the world upside down; it will be said of the apostles soon to be anointed that they have turned an upside down world right side up. Nations will tremble at the mention of their name, but they will also be healed by them.

The magnitude of the troubles or the revival cannot be adequately expressed here. I have only been given to see a small part of the actual unfolding of these events. As stated in the introduction, I did not see the end, but my vision ended with increasing chaos and increasing revival. More of this revelation will be given in due time. We should now concern ourselves with the preparation for this great harvest. We must seek the Lord for his strategy and vision, and give ourselves completely to His purposes.

There will be other words and exhortations, originating from the very throne of the Lord and carrying great authority, coming to prepare His church for the days to come. Not to presume this will be all that He will be saying, but we will soon hear His prophets and teachers begin to emphasize the following:

1. BUILD UPON THE ONLY FOUNDATION THAT CAN BE LAID. JESUS HIMSELF. Works that are built upon truths instead of The Truth will not stand in this day. Many congregations and ministries are today devastated by the slightest shaking. The works that are properly built on a relationship with Jesus will withstand the greatest trials and attacks without being moved. There will be a great emphasis on the Lord Jesus Himself in the days to come. The increasing revelation of Him will overshadow the many emphases of the past like the greater light of the sun overshadows the lessor light of the moon when it rises. The truths that have been such a distraction will begin to seem insignificant as the church begins to see Him "in whom are hidden ALL of the treasures of wisdom and knowledge" (Col.2:3).

2. REMOVE THE BARRIERS AND FACADES THAT SEPARATE US FROM THE LORD AND EACH OTHER. We must become more intimate with Him, and through Him, with each other. Spiritual pride and the exaltation of men, individual truths, or works, will come under unrelenting discipline from the Lord and will soon be understood as

"strange fire". Those who continue to offer it will perish from the ministry with such demonstration that a pure and holy fear of the Lord will sweep the Body of Christ. This will help the church to move into true spiritual worship and a unity that is based on that worship.

3. ABIDE IN THE SABBATH REST OF THE LORD. This will become an increasing emphasis and a reality as the Lord enters His temple, the church. Our growing intimacy with Him will bring a peace that will actually calm the storm of the rising sea of humanity. The intensity of the times will overwhelm any pseudo peace. We must be one with the "Lord of the Sabbath."

4. HEED THE SPIRITUAL PREPARATION WHICH MAY BE REFLECTED IN THE NATURAL. For example: Some have begun moving their assets into precious metals or land. This may be helpful, but it is far more important to take the spiritual land and to lay up our treasures in heaven. The Lord is seeking givers who will become channels of His supply. For these there will not be any lack. Those that hoard or do not learn to freely give may suffer increasing crisis in their earthly affairs. This is the Lord's discipline to set them free. Some who are faithful and generous givers may also experience increasing crisis in this, but it is for their preparation to become channels for the provision of many. Remember Joseph!

Some are feeling they should limit their travel to certain areas and are beginning to emphasize personal hygiene because of the AIDS epidemic. This may be helpful to a degree, but the only true deliverance from the judgments of God is to be found in Christ. Spiritual purity will automatically result in natural purity, and is far more important. It alone will protect us from AIDS or any other plague.

5. "THE JUST SHALL LIVE BY FAITH," NOT FEAR. Fears will greatly increase in the world. Actions taken by the church because of fear will almost always prove destructive. Some "faith teaching" has muddied the waters to the degree that some do not even want to hear the word "faith." This

frequently happens before the Lord begins a great work. A great revelation of true faith is coming; it will be an essential revelation for us to serve in these days. Some will be called to walk where angels fear to tread. KNOW that He who is in us is MUCH greater than he who is in the world. The vessels He is now preparing will walk in a boldness and confidence that will astonish a world gripped in fear. Our faith will grow as the presence of the Lord increases. True faith is the recognition of the One in whom we believe. When one truly and properly fears the Lord he will not fear anything else.

In the coming days many will exist in the miraculous on a continual basis. This will become as natural to them as the gathering of manna was to Israel. Some of the Lord's exploits on behalf of His people will be unprecedented, exceeding the greatest Biblical miracles. These will seem almost normal as they take place because the presence of the Lord will cause more wonderment than His works. He will be very close to His people in these days.

6. THE LORD WILL SOON OPEN OUR UNDER-STANDING OF HIS WORD AND PURPOSES TO A DEPTH BEYOND OUR PRESENT COMPREHENSION. The "books" are yet to be "opened" as they will be. When they are our understanding of even basic truths, such as salvation, being born again, etc.. will be enormously increased. This will give far more substance and depth of purpose to the entire body of Christ. The functions of the gifts and ministries will come with increasing authority and power as their confidence increases with knowledge. The spiritual dimension will become more real to the church than the natural. When the proper Foundation has been adequately laid in the church (our union and devotion to Jesus Himself) the Spirit of Revelation will be poured out as never before.

There have been many notable outpourings of the Holy Spirit, but there has always been little lasting fruit. Multitudes who met the Lord were lost again to the world; but the Lord did accomplish what He intended. Many of those brought into the kingdom remained and matured. He now has what will prove to be a strong foundation on which to build, a net to hold the catch that He has prepared for the end of the age. Through the tribulations and dry times of the last few years He has carefully been weaving strong cords that He is now beginning to bind together.

Do not resist the Lord in this work. Seek greater intimacy with the Lord and open yourself to your fellow members in the body of Christ. Reach out to them and remove the barriers. Those who have drifted into extremes will be brought back to the course never again to be distracted from the River of Life by the little tributaries which feed it. Those who have resisted new truth will soon be diving into the River, fearless of rocks or depths. The anointing will soon break all of our yokes. The Reformation showed us the Way. The Pentecostal and Charismatic renewals began leading us on to Truth. Through the coming revival we will begin to know Jesus as our Life. When the cord has all three strands it will not be broken again.

This word is given for the PREPARATION of those whom the Lord desires to use. Relationships are about to be built between ministries and congregations that have feared and rejected each other in the past. He will do this in many without changing their doctrines or emphasis; He will merely cause His people to rise above such differences and worship Him in unity. As He is lifted up we will gradually begin to wonder how many concerns that were so important to us, and often divided us, could have had so much of our attention. As this final battle begins we are all going to be amazed, and sometimes ashamed, at those we find on our side.

It is more important to abide in Him day by day than to foresee the things which are to come. If we are abiding in Him we will be at the right place and well prepared for all that He has given us to do. Jesus did not come to show us the way, He came to BE the Way. The Holy Spirit was not sent to give us guidance, He came to BE our Guide. Deception is not just misunderstanding truth, it is not being in His will. Regardless of how accurate our vision and knowledge of the times are, if we are not in His will we can be in serious trouble. We must seek the Lord, not for what we are to do, but because HE IS WHAT WE SHOULD DO. He is the Ark given for our salvation.

This vision is not intended to advocate a great emphasis upon the future and eschatology, but rather the awareness and determination of the church not to waste a single day in drawing near to God. All of our knowledge and speculation about Armageddon will not do us any good if we meet our Armageddon at the stop light on the way to work. In the days to come it will not matter too much what we know, but Who we know, and how well we know Him. As the Lord Himself exhorted us, we must not be ignorant of the signs of the times, but it is of far greater importance to know the One who is in control of all of these things, and to be found doing His will.

If we are to know His voice we must know Him. I once read an account of three shepherds who simultaneously brought their sheep to a watering hole. The herds mingled until it was impossible to tell them apart. The shepherds seemed unconcerned though it appeared that they might never be able to get the sheep sorted out again. When it was time for them to depart each shepherd took a different path and began to sing as he went. There was a huge convulsion in the mixed herd; then little streams of sheep began to follow after each shepherd until they had all separated. Though all of the shepherds were singing, they each knew their own shepherd's voice.

There are many voices in the world each leading down different paths. All of the paths look good, but there is only one way that leads to life. We cannot follow a path; if we are walking by formulas and "how to's" we will easily be mislead. We must follow Him. We must be able to distinguish His voice from all of the others even when they are all clamoring for our attention. It is not enough to know someone, or to be following someone who does know His voice. Many who are in leadership will have been removed. We must each know Him for ourselves. We must each be intimate with Him. When Job lost everything but the Lord he then understood that he didn't need anything but the Lord. Neither do we! He is everything that we need for these times and for all time.

Humble yourself under His mighty hand so that you may take part in a great exaltation. Those who allow themselves to be emptied, who lay aside all personal ambition to become of no reputation, who patiently suffer rejection and misunderstanding, will soon stir the entire world with the King's message.

We have a kingdom which cannot be shaken. This kingdom is so great, so powerful, that if all of the greatest problems and tragedies were afflicted upon it at once, it may not even be enough to get the attention of a single inhabitant. In the awesome expanse of God's universe, the entire earth compares as less than a single drop of water to all of the worlds oceans. Except for this tiny little speck called earth, the goodness of God dominates the universe. He is in control.

The power He has given to the least of His little ones is greater than all of the power of the enemy--He has given us His Son. The whole creation does, and always will, marvel at what He has done for us, but we seem almost oblivious to it. It is time for us to awaken. It is time for us to come to know and abide in the One who dwells within us. He must become more real to us than all of the earths problems or attractions. Once we see Him, and the kingdom He has given to us, nothing on earth will again distract us. When we see our King, all human pomp and position seems pitifully insignificant. When we see Him that which is eternal becomes more real to us than that which is passing away. In this way our lives are steered irresistibly towards the city which has foundations; the one whose Architect AND Builder is God.

THE VISION OF

MORNINGSTAR PUBLICATIONS, INC.

It is the purpose of MPI to:

#1 Promulgate important teachings and timely prophetic messages to the church.

#2 Promote interchange between the different streams in the body of Christ. We feel called to pursue this in the following ways:

1) Sponsor Conferences In Strategic Cities. This is to provide a platform for anointed ministries to impart to integated assemblies, and to provide a setting for relationships to begin and grow. From these we expect the spawning of regular leadership meetings (both local and extra-local), prophetic conferences, intercessory prayer groups, etc...

2) Use The Morning Star Prophetic Newsletter as a channel of interchange by relating significant events in the church, distributing important teachings and prophetic words, and giving notice of important meetings which are open to the whole body.

AND TO ESTABLISH:

3) A TEACHING CENTER where those with a timely message will be invited to minister for various periods of time. When appropriate, their messages will be recorded and published for distribution.

4) A HOUSE OF PROPHETS to be located with the Teaching Center. This will be a place where mature prophets can gather to seek the Lord for the unity and clarity of vision which will be required in the days to come.
A mandate for calling these two ministries together is to develop the necessary interchange between them. As the

prophets and teachers at Antioch ministered to the Lord TOGETHER it resulted in the birth of powerful ministries and apostolic teams. We are expecting the same.

5) A SABBATH REST CENTER to provide for ministries who have served in the field for extended periods of time. Here they will be able to just seek the Lord for up to one year. We expect this to result in a greater clarity of vision and increased anointing, for these ministers, and thereby to the whole body of Christ.

6) A PUBLISHING CENTER to include all of the equipment and facilities needed for publishing books, tapes, newsletters, videos, etc., of the highest quality for distribution.

7) A CHANNEL OF SUPPORT FOR APOSTOLIC TEAMS to include intercessory prayer, spiritual covering, financial support and housing for the families of those called to the field for extended periods.

8) A SUPPORT COMMUNITY to be made up of those who are committed to the service of the Center, and the families of those sent out by them. These will also form a local congregation for the functioning of the gifts and ministries required for the equipping of those who are called to this work.

If you would like to help in the support of this work, receive The Morning Star prophetic newsletter, or our catalog of books and tapes, our address is:

MORNINGSTAR PUBLICATIONS, INC.
8704-C PAULSTON ROAD
CHARLOTTE, NORTH CAROLINA 28226

Morningstar Publications, Inc. is organized as a non-profit corporation. All contributions are tax deductable We appreciate your encouragement and support.